FROM THE OUTSIDE LOOKING IN

D1051417

FROM THE
OUTSIDE
LOOKING
IN

Short Stories for LDS Teenagers

EDITED BY

CHRIS CROWE

Bookcraft
Salt Lake City, Utah

For Jonathan, my friend and my son

Library of Congress Catalog Card Number 98-71544
ISBN 1-57008-412-2

First Printing, 1998

Printed in the United States of America

CONTENTS

Testimony

Decisions

ACKNOWLEDGMENTS

Some of the stories in this book appear by permission of the *New Era*. Most of the writers in this collection of short stories owe a debt of gratitude to Brian Kelly, former editor of the *New Era*, and to Richard Romney, current editor of the *New Era*, for the support they received as fledgling fiction writers.

"Wallflower," by Louise Plummer
"The Girl with the All-American Teeth," by Ann Edwards Cannon
"The Most Important Thing" (On the Inside Looking In),
by Jack Weyland
"Sink or Swim," by Adrian R. Gostick
"A Light Still Burning," by Alma J. Yates
© The Church of Jesus Christ of Latter-day Saints
Previously published in the *New Era*
Used by permission

FROM THE OUTSIDE LOOKING IN

THIS BOOK CONTAINS FIFTEEN SHORT STORIES written especially for Latter-day Saint teenagers. Each of the authors was given the challenge to write an interesting, honest short story that was uplifting without being preachy. The authors' other challenge was to write a story that fit the theme: "From the outside looking in."

What does it mean to be from the outside looking in?

It means to feel—or to be—out of it, left out, alienated, alone, or abandoned. Excluded or shunned. Different or peculiar. Nearly all kids feel peculiar at one time or another, but because you're LDS you may at times feel even more "peculiar" than most teenagers. Of course, if you've paid much attention in seminary you know that in the scriptural context *peculiar* doesn't mean "weird," it means "unique." And it's OK to be peculiar-unique.

But when you're a teenager, it's hard not to feel peculiar-weird sometimes. And being LDS may make you feel even more peculiar-weird. While everybody else you know is "having fun," you're not. You might be the only one who can't drink, date, and stay out all night, the only one who has parents who insist on certain standards and rules, the only one with a large family, or the only one planning to go on a mission. Because it's not always easy for friends of other faiths to understand your beliefs and standards, you may feel alienated from or even rejected by them.

But there are times even within your Church world when you may feel like an outsider. It might seem that everyone but you has a strong testimony. Or maybe you're the only kid in your ward with divorced parents. Or the only one whose parents aren't active. Or the only one who seems to feel intimidated about going on a mission. Or the only one who has no athletic talent. Life isn't easy for anyone—teenager or adult, member or not. Membership in The Church of Jesus Christ of Latter-day Saints is not a guarantee that you'll never have problems. As President Gordon B. Hinckley recently said in a Churchwide satellite broadcast, "We still have problems, many of them."

Problems are an inevitable part of life for everyone, but being a member of the Church can help you find answers to the questions and difficulties of adolescence that make you feel like an outsider.

The stories in this collection show kids, maybe some kids like you, facing tough times and wrestling with a wide range of problems. Their challenges make them feel alone, even abandoned. In one way or another, they're all on the outside looking in. With the help of friends, family, and faith in the Lord, the characters in these stories manage to find peace and their place in the world.

one

Fathers
Relationships
Testimony
Decisions

Have you ever felt really out of it at a dance?
Lonely? Bored? Ignored?
The narrator in this story does, but she gets rescued in a surprising way.

WALLFLOWER

Louise Plummer

YES, I LOOK GOOD. I LOOK REALLY GREAT, as a matter of fact. I needn't worry about anything. I look sensational in this red dress. Red looks best on me, and I look sensational. Except for the buttons. I don't like the buttons Mother picked. They're really crummy buttons. But if I hold up my arm in front like this, no one will see them there. Now I really do look sensational, and no one can see the buttons at all. I feel the music. I'm with it. It's going to work for me tonight. Positive thinking will work. It will. It will.

There's Herb Blakely. He's looking at me. He likes my dress. I can tell. He took a step toward me. I'll bet he wants to dance with me, but he's afraid to ask. I'll smile at him. Come across the room, Herbie, and ask me to dance. Tell me I look sensational. Ask me to dance, Herbie. The power of positive thinking is at work. Ask me, Herbie. Ask me. You jerk! He'll be back, maybe. I'm sure he looked at me. Herbie likes me. He said "Hi" in Sunday School last week. That's all he said, but I could tell by the way he said it that he likes me. He said "Hi" and then walked past me. But I could tell it meant something.

If I don't stand by any other girls, someone will ask me to dance. Oh my gosh, here comes Martha Bluke. Go away, Martha. Go away. Don't stand here by me. Go away, Martha. The power of positive thinking. It worked! I can't believe it. She went over to the corner with Mary Anne Little and Beth Kelly. They're dancing with each other! Oh, I can't stand it. Three girls dancing in a corner. Gross.

3

Oh, there's Ralph. I'll smile a little more. He's so darling. Really. He is so cool. He looked at me. My mouth hurts from smiling, and my arm hurts too. Crummy buttons. Tell me I'm witty and cute, Ralph. Oh Ralph, you could make my entire adolescence if you'd just ask me to dance. Ask me, Ralph. Ask me. He asked Lila Kirk. Bozo. Look how close they're dancing. Isn't anyone going to break them up? I would never dance that close with anyone. Not with anyone.

Except maybe Chuck Stewart. I just adore him. He's so sweet. He always stands with his hands in his pockets. I really like that. And his hair covers his ears in a really delicious way, and I think he shaves. I'll bet he's the only boy in this entire ward who shaves. Mmmm, there he is. I can't breathe. If I could dance with Chuck Stewart, I'd never ask for another thing in my entire life. I'm smiling at him, and I've got all my buttons covered, and he's looking at me. I winked at him! How could I wink at him? It was an accident. I winked at Chuck Stewart. I must have a tic. I've never in my life done that. He'll think I'm weird. Oh Chuck, I didn't mean to wink at you like a creep. He asked Martha. Martha! How could he ask her? She was dancing with all those girls, and he asked her. It was because I winked, I'll bet. He'd rather ask a girl who dances with girls than a girl who winks. I must have a tic. Martha thinks she dances so well.

Roger Humphries! I thought he'd moved out of the ward. Oh, wow! Oh, neato! Look at the way he chews his gum. Let me chew your gum, Roger. He's walking across the dance floor. I can't breathe. My arm is going to sleep. Positive thinking. Positive thinking. Ask me—ask me—ask me. Oh Roger, you are so *numero uno* neato!

He's looking at me. My lips are quivering. They're quivering. My palms are beginning to perspire. Gross. He's coming right toward me. My mouth hurts. My arm. My crummy buttons. Why didn't I wear something else? Ask me, Roger. Ask me to dance. Tell me that I'm the best-looking thing you've seen all night. Tell me I'm beautiful and charming and witty and exciting and that you've had your eye on me for years. Tell me you love me, Roger. Or just ask me to dance!

Don't walk past me. He's drinking red punch. Why not red dress? Me? Oh pooh, who cares? I don't. I really don't. To think I came to this crummy dance when I could be home reading *The Scarlet Letter.*

My father! My father the bishop is walking toward me. No, Daddy, no. No. Please don't. Please go to the punch bowl. No, Daddy, don't smile so lovingly at me. Oh, please let me be struck dead instantly. He says I'm the most beautiful thing he's seen all evening. Would I dance just one with him? He says I'm exciting and charming and witty and that I dance like Ginger Rogers, who-ever she is. He says he loves me.

Oh, Daddy, I love you too.

Louise Plummer lives in Salt Lake City with her husband, Tom. They both work at BYU; he teaches German and she teaches creative writing. She is the author of three award-winning novels for teenagers: *The Romantic Obsessions and Humiliations of Annie Sehlmeier; My Name is Sus5an Smith. The 5 is Silent;* and *The Unlikely Romance of Kate Bjorkman.* In addition to her young adult novels, she has also published a col-lection of essays for LDS readers called *Thoughts of a Grasshopper.* "Wallflower" was her first published short story. She has nearly completed a new novel called *Hannah Ziebarth at Large.*

It's nice to have the priesthood in the home.
When you're sick or troubled, you can ask your father for a blessing.
But what if your father isn't "worthy" to give a blessing?

THE GIRL WITH THE ALL-AMERICAN TEETH

Ann Edwards Cannon

AS IF BEING A KID ISN'T BAD ENOUGH. I had to grow up next door to the girl with the all-American teeth. Allison Adamson had the straightest, whitest teeth in the history of orthodontics. Adults always commented on this. Every time they got together, you could count on them to say, "Doesn't the Adamson girl have lovely teeth?"

As for me, I was more interested in the fact that Allison took tap, tumbling, ballet, baton, and hula lessons after school. She also played the piano and collected dolls from different countries. Best of all, she had her own dog—a white poodle named Hercules. Me, I just had a goldfish named Ralph. You can probably see already how things were for me growing up next door to someone like Allison Adamson.

Because we were neighbors who happened to be LDS, Allison and I ended up doing things together all the time. During the summer we went to the pool with Allison's mom, and during the winter we watched cartoons after school together. This made everyone think, of course, that we were best friends, and we were. Sort of.

The problem was that underneath all my smiles I was jealous of Allison. I wanted all the pretty girl things she had that my parents couldn't buy for me. I wanted them so badly that my chest literally hurt at times. I wanted her dolls, her canopy bed with the foamy pink bedspread, her play makeup case with the play makeup. I can remember sitting in her white wicker rocker one day and telling her I'd trade my shoebox of Bazooka bubble-gum wrappers for one of her bendable Barbies. She wasn't interested, of course.

Years ago, as our eighth birthdays were coming up in April, one day on the way home from school Allison asked who was going to baptize me.

I hadn't thought about it much. "I don't know," I confessed. "Who's going to baptize you?"

"My dad," she said proudly.

"Well, I guess my dad will baptize me too, then," I told her. I'd never seen anyone baptized—I'm the oldest in my family—but I figured my dad could probably do it if someone showed him how.

Allison looked at me with wide, disbelieving blue eyes. "But he can't!" she exclaimed. This was news to me. "Why?" I wanted to know.

"Because my mom says he can't. My mom says he isn't worthy."

I didn't know what the word *worthy* meant, but I didn't like Allison's tone. "Yes he is too worthy," I said.

"No he's not."

"Yes he is."

Allison stopped and stared at me the way our third-grade teacher always stared at stupid Stewart Lufgren. "Your dad is not worthy, Brenda, because he doesn't go to church and he smokes. I know he smokes because I can smell it when I go to your house." She wrinkled her little button nose in distaste. "Don't you know *anything?*"

My throat suddenly felt very tight. Blood was pounding in my ears. "I hate you, Allison Adamson," I said finally. Then I turned and ran home.

Our house is so busy with people that at first no one noticed how miserable I was. At dinner, though, Mom squinted her eyes at me and said across the table, "Are you OK, Brenda honey?"

I nodded yes.

She came into my bedroom that night before I fell asleep. "Did something happen to you at school today, Brenda? You can tell me about it if you want to."

"No, nothing happened," I answered, as tonelessly as a telephone operator.

Mom just sat there on the foot of my bed for a minute. Then she said, "Do you want to talk to Daddy?" Sometimes I told him things I wouldn't tell anybody else. But this time I shook my head. Hard.

"No!"

I laid awake in bed for a long time that night watching shadows skip across my wall. Yessir, Allison had it all: extra money for Weekly Reader paperbacks, a locket with pictures inside, and a father who could baptize her.

That was the first time I realized that my dad was different. I mean I always knew he didn't go to church, but that hadn't added up to anything—you think your father is just like everybody else's dad when you're a kid. But Allison had opened my eyes. The day we were baptized, Allison, looking like she had just stepped out of a fairy tale in her long, white gown, was taken into the font by her smiling father. I was baptized by my Uncle Bill. Dad sat in the congregation looking uncomfortable in a suit. His rough, brown worker's hands were folded in his lap.

Things changed some between my father and me after that. Not that you could tell by looking at us—he still teased and tickled me and called me Sport, and I still begged him to take me to baseball games. For sure we loved each other. But I didn't tell him private things anymore. And then, too, I started noticing all the ways he wasn't worthy. I didn't want to, but I couldn't help myself.

If things changed between my father and me then, they changed even more between Allison and me. By the time we were freshmen in high school, we had pretty much gone our separate ways. Allison went from honors class to honors class while I wore an army jacket and hung around the library with this nice but weird group of kids who all wanted to be science-fiction writers when they grew up. Although she thought my friends were bad enough, it was the army jacket that really got to Allison.

"Only our boys in the armed forces should wear khaki," she used to say.

And now this year, the girl with the all-American teeth and I are taking early-morning seminary together. There are two teachers, Brother Marshall and Brother Phillips. Brother Marshall is

Mormondom's answer to Robert Redford. All jawbone and blond hair, Brother Marshall is gorgeous. He lettered in about a million sports when he was in college, so you can see he's athletic, too. Besides this he's young, nice, smart, and very funny. All the kids love him. Brother Phillips, on the other hand, is old enough to have fought in World War II. He's small and stooped, just like a little gnome, and when he talks he whispers.

Funny thing, though: I like Brother Phillips best. I like the way he listens carefully to your questions, then thinks for a while before he answers. And lots of times he'll answer, "I don't know." This drives Allison crazy. "If he wants to teach seminary then he should know," she says. Maybe he should. I can't say. I just like the way he seems so thoughtful about things.

The reason I'm even telling you all this is that I have a problem. I'm not talking about your typical teenager problems of losing books, being ambushed by a gang of pimples the night before a dance, or dropping lunch trays. No. This one is a red-alert problem. Next Tuesday morning I have to check into the hospital for a series of tests. They say I've got a tumor of some sort.

Frankly, I'm scared.

I thought some sort of blessing might help. I don't mean a blessing that promises I'll get better or anything like that. Just one that makes me feel like I'm not going through this alone. I thought maybe I'd ask Brother Phillips if he'd give me one; there's something fatherly about him.

I feel pretty silly, actually, standing here at Brother Phillips's office door. This is not the sort of thing I usually do. But I want a blessing.

I knock.

"Come in, come in." Brother Phillips opens his door and greets me. When he smiles, his cheeks turn into small apples.

"How are you, Brenda?" he asks.

"OK," I reply, looking around his office. It's the first time I've ever been inside. It's filled with books and old family pictures of people who look like characters on *Leave It to Beaver* reruns. His children, I think, must be all grown up and gone away by now. Did they ever ask him for blessings?

"What can I do for you?" he asks after inviting me to sit down.

Now that I'm here, I feel really stupid. I don't know how to ask him for what I want. "Well," I begin, "I'm going into the hospital Tuesday morning."

Brother Phillips draws his bristle-brush brows together in concern. Encouraged by his silent sympathy, I go on. "Anyway, I want to know if you would mind giving me a blessing or something. It doesn't have to be long or fancy."

Brother Phillips looks at me for a moment, then presses his fingertips together and leans back in his swivel chair.

"I could do that," he says slowly.

I wait. He doesn't move.

"Brenda," he says finally, "have you asked your father to give you a blessing?"

This is certainly a ball of the curved variety. I'm taken totally by surprise. "Well, no," I confess.

"I see." Pause. "Do you think perhaps you ought to go to him before you come to me?"

I can't believe this. Brother Phillips knows that my father isn't active in the Church.

"I don't know," I begin to stammer. "I guess I just thought that—" The memory of Allison, her perfect little mouth forming the words *not worthy,* jumps up like a puppet before my eyes, and with it the same old feelings of shame and rage return for an encore. "My father can't give me a blessing!" I blurt out.

Brother Phillips shrugs. "Well, maybe not a formal blessing. But every parent has a prayer for his child. Go home, Brenda. Ask your father to tell you what's in his heart for you. I know your father. He's a good man."

I leave feeling embarrassed, even a little angry that I didn't get what I came for. All the same, though, I feel oddly comforted. Brother Phillips's words *I know your father* play reel-to-reel through my mind.

Yes. And I know my father, too. I've lived with him for sixteen years. I've seen him talk silly to the babies, play Candyland with my brothers without looking bored, and scream at me to stay away from a live wire. I think he's the kind of man who would have a prayer for his children.

Allison is standing at the bus stop looking perfect. I'll say this for all those baton lessons: they sure gave Allison good posture.

"Hi, Allison," I say, joining her.

"Hi, Brenda."

We don't say anything for a minute. Then she says, "I'm really sorry that you have to go to the hospital." I can tell by looking at her face that she does feel bad. I smile at her.

"Me too."

"Is there anything I can do to help?"

I think about this for a minute. Then I shake my head.

She drops her voice so none of the other kids will hear. "I'll say a prayer for you, at least."

"Yes," I say slowly. "A prayer would be nice."

Ann Edwards Cannon lives in Salt Lake City with her husband, Ken, and their five sons: Philip, Alec, Dylan, Geoffrey, and Quinton. She currently writes a weekly column for the *Deseret News,* a regular column for *This People* magazine, and scripts for "Music and the Spoken Word." In addition to articles and short stories she has published, she is the author of three award-winning novels for teenagers: *Cal Cameron by Day, Spiderman by Night, Shadow Brothers,* and *Amazing Gracie.*

Lorraine is reluctant to confront a painful reality. With the loving support of her "family," she's able to abandon her fantasy and face the unpleasant truth about her father.

A PENCIL NAMED BOB

Lael Littke

I FOUND THE PENCIL ON THE SAME DAY that the package came from my dad. It was lying on the sidewalk outside the elementary school where I'd stopped to wait for Philip Atterbury, who is the son of Thelma Atterbury, my temporary mother.

Normally I wouldn't pick up a pencil from the street. I mean, fourteen-year-old girls don't go around harvesting stuff off the sidewalk. Besides, if I needed a pencil I'd just write to my dad and he'd send me one. He'd send me a dozen if I asked him to.

But this pencil was like those holograms that change colors depending on which way you look at them. It was different.

Like me.

Forget I said that. I'll be back to being like everybody else soon, the way I used to be.

When I picked up the pencil, I saw the name *Bob* printed on it. Most pencils I've met have been yellow and say Dixon Ticonderoga or Eberhard Faber on them. This one just said BOB.

My dad's name is Bob.

It had to be a sign. I was going to hear from Dad. Or he was going to send for me to come and live with him. Or maybe I'd get a letter saying he was coming back and we could just go on living there in Forest Hill, which would be fine with me. Maybe we could even live in our old house again, and I'd put up our Families Are Forever poster right where it used to be.

Philip Atterbury and about a thousand other wild beasts came stampeding out of the schoolhouse just then, so I shoved the pencil into my backpack. Philip Atterbury doesn't mind being called a wild beast. In fact, he likes it. He's only five, a kindergartner. Which is why I have to stop on my way home from middle school to walk with him.

"Hi," Philip Atterbury said. "Who are you this week?"

It's a game we play. He wants me to call him by his whole name, Philip Atterbury. Actually he has a middle name—Chester—but he says I don't need to use that. Then he will call me by whatever name I've chosen for the week. I always write it at the top of my notebook.

"Phoenix," I said. I held up my notebook for him to see the name, even though he can't read that well yet.

A little thrill ran through me because I'd chosen Phoenix as my name of the week before I found the pencil named Bob. Didn't that, plus the pencil, add up for sure to my dad getting in touch with me? I mean, I chose Phoenix because it's a mythical bird that rises from its own ashes. And that's what I was going to do as soon as my dad sent for me.

My life pretty much burned down three years ago when my mom died and my dad dumped me. Well, he didn't really dump me. What he said was, "Rain, I can't hack this being a single parent. I have to go away for a while."

When I said it would take me only five minutes to pack, he said, "Eleven-year-old girls need to be in school. I'm going to be moving around with a construction job in Alaska. I'll send for you when I find a permanent place for us to live."

I said I'd be happy to live in an igloo, as long as it was with him, but he didn't even answer that. He just left me with Thelma Atterbury, who'd been a friend of my mom's, and took off.

That was three years ago.

"Phoenix," Philip Atterbury said. "That's pretty. "FEEEEEEEN-ix. What does it mean?"

"It's a city in Arizona," I told him. What did he know about mythical birds rising from their own ashes?

We walked along talking about FEEEEEN-ix, which he said sounded like a town where there'd be lots of KLEEEEN-ex. I said Boise—BOY-see—sounded like a place where there'd be lots of

JOY-see, and we both giggled. Philip Atterbury doesn't know where Boise is, or even *what* it is, but he laughed anyway.

Thelma wasn't home when we got there, but the package was. The package from my dad. So the pencil *had* been a sign.

His name was up in the corner. There was no return address.

Wasn't that just like him to forget to put it on? He'd probably enclosed a letter inside with the address and maybe even directions as to how I could find him.

Philip Atterbury touched the package. "What's that?"

"Just a package from my dad," I said. "He's always sending me stuff."

"Since when?" Philip Atterbury asked.

Well, maybe it was the first package I'd gotten from him, but he'd sent me a Christmas card the year before.

"Is it for your birthday?" Philip Atterbury asked.

"My birthday is in October," I said. "This is April." I thought about it. "So maybe it's an early birthday present."

"Open it," Philip Atterbury instructed.

I opened it. Inside was a pair of moose house slippers. You know, big furry ones with antlers.

"Wow," Philip Atterbury said. "I wish I had a dad who would send me a neat present like that."

Philip Atterbury's dad is dead, like my mom. In fact, they were killed in the same car accident. My dad and Thelma were in the car, too, but they weren't hurt too badly.

I looked in the box for the letter with my dad's address and directions for getting where he was.

Except for the slippers, the box was empty.

I kicked off my shoes and put the moose slippers on my feet.

"Wow," Philip Atterbury said again. He got down and put his face against the soft furriness.

OK, so there wasn't any note. It was all right. Dad had to love me to send me a terrific present like the moose slippers. He'd be writing me a letter any day now.

Which reminded me of the pencil in my backpack.

I fished it out.

"What's that?" Philip Atterbury asked.

"A pencil. You know what a pencil is, don't you?"

He giggled.

"It's named Bob." I showed him. "B-O-B. That spells Bob."

I didn't tell him it was my dad's name. He didn't remember my dad. He didn't even remember *his* dad.

There were a couple of tooth marks in the wood of the pencil.

I rubbed my finger over the marks. The pencil was like me. It had been chewed up a little, too.

Sitting down at the kitchen table, I pulled a notebook from my backpack, tore out a page, and started writing with the pencil.

Dear Phoenix, I wrote.

No, my dad wouldn't know I was Phoenix that week.

I erased it and wrote, *Dear Rain.*

Actually, my name is Lorraine, but Dad always called me Rain. He's the only one who can use that name. I mean, the reason I choose a different name each week is that I'm waiting for my dad to come back and recognize the only true me. Of course I have to have an official name for school records and stuff like that, so I use Lorraine for that. But my friends look at my notebook each Monday morning to see what my name of the week is, and they call me that.

Dear Rain, I wrote. *It's cold here in Alaska, but I have a warm cabin that's just waiting for you and that Families Are Forever poster of yours. I'm sending money next week to pay for your plane trip up here.*

Or would I go by train? I didn't know how a person got to Alaska.

I was still thinking about that when Thelma came home.

Thelma is a hairdresser and stands up all day long, so the first thing she did after hugging Philip Atterbury was flop onto the sofa and put her feet on the coffee table.

"So how did *your* day go, hon?" she asked me.

It's no big deal to be called "hon" by Thelma. She calls everybody "hon." She says it to the mailman and to the woman on the phone who calls each month to see if we have any old clothes to donate and to the brown dog next door who wags his tail when he sees her coming.

"Fine." I folded the paper I'd been writing on and shoved the pencil into my backpack again.

"Doing your homework already?" Thelma asked.

"No," I said. "This is a letter."

"Who from?"

"Bob wrote it," I said.

I don't know why I said that. It wasn't a lie, exactly. But I didn't feel good about it.

I looked to see if Philip Atterbury had heard what I'd said. He was busy going through Thelma's purse, looking for the piece of butterscotch candy she took from the pink dish in the beauty parlor every day and squirreled away in her purse for him.

"Bob?" Thelma's forehead wrinkled. "Since when do you call your dad Bob? Or is it some other Bob?"

"No," I said.

She took that to mean no, it wasn't some other Bob. "You mean he finally remembered he has a daughter back here in Forest Hill?"

"He sent me these." I held up my feet in the moose slippers. I was on solid ground here. He *had* sent the slippers.

"Cute," Thelma said. "What did he say in the letter?"

"Not much." I needed to change the subject. "Did Howard come by today?"

Howard was a guy Thelma liked. She was always saying that what we needed was a man around the house to make us a family. "We're just a bunch of looky-loos," she'd say, "gawking into the windows of all those dad-and-mom-and-kids families."

Actually, I was the looky-loo, gawking through the window at her and Philip Atterbury. At least *they* were related.

"No, hon," Thelma said. "He didn't come by. This is the ninth day he hasn't come by." And she changed the subject as abruptly as I'd done. "What should we do for family home evening tonight?"

Philip Atterbury immediately started suggesting things to do, like watching the Wallace and Gromit video he'd gotten for his birthday or playing Chutes and Ladders at the kitchen table.

I gathered up my stuff. "I'll hurry and do my homework."

Mainly I just wanted to get away before Thelma questioned me any more about the fake Bob letter.

In my room I unfolded it again and pulled the pencil from my backpack.

At the end of the letter I added, *P.S. I love you, Rain.*

Then I opened my math book.

I didn't get a letter from my dad the next day, the next, or the next. And Howard didn't come by the beauty parlor to see Thelma that day, either. Not the next, or the next.

On Thursday she came home and said Howard had just gotten engaged to Angela Farnsworth, one of the other hairdressers in Thelma's shop. He'd met her when he came in to visit Thelma.

"It's all right," Thelma said.

But maybe it wasn't all right. What about the dad-and-mom-and-kids family Thelma talked about?

It seemed like Gloom City around her house.

Except for that pencil named Bob.

It wrote another message to me.

We've really been busy here at my job in Alaska, it wrote. *Night and day. But that means I'm racking up big bucks. How would you like a red convertible for your sixteenth birthday?*

I signed it, *Snowed in with love.*

I wasn't really blaming it on the pencil. I mean, it was *my* hand controlling it.

I wished I could control my dad like I could the pencil.

I added a P.S. *How is Thelma these days?*

Wouldn't it be neat if Dad came back and married Thelma? Then she could forget about Howard, and she and Dad and Philip Atterbury and I could be a family. Then we'd be like everybody else.

I stuck the letter in my backpack because I didn't want it lying around the house for Thelma to find.

The trouble was, the next day when I pulled out my literature book during English class the letter came with it, falling on the floor in front of my desk. My best friend, Ardean Belmont, swooped down to pick it up.

"Hey," she said. "What are you keeping from me? Who's Bob?"

She wasn't being especially snoopy, but she couldn't help seeing the letter because it fell flat, with the written side up.

"My dad's name is Bob," I said.

"You heard from your dad, Phoenix?" Ardean scanned the letter again. "Yipes! A convertible! You're kidding!"

I took the sheet of paper from her. "My sixteenth birthday is almost two years away." I looked around to see if anybody else had heard.

They had. Tammy Sykes zoomed over and snatched the paper. "First dibs on rides," she yipped.

Others came over to hear, and pretty soon everybody in the class knew I'd gotten a letter from my dad saying he was buying me a red convertible.

"It's just a maybe," I said weakly. "It's two years away."

It didn't seem to matter.

By the end of the day about sixty kids were signed up to ride in my red convertible.

And by Sunday, all the kids at church knew about it, too. That was bad news.

I mean, it was bad enough at school, but at church? Where all the time we're having lessons on honesty and singing "Do What Is Right." Would I have to give my CTR ring back?

Things got worse.

It was fast Sunday, when the Young Men and Young Women groups meet together. We had a speaker who talked about keeping a journal, which was a pretty safe subject, but then it was testimony time and Sister Clifford, our Young Women president, tossed the testimony bear to me first thing.

The testimony bear is just something to get us to stand up and talk. It's a big teddy bear that one of the leaders tosses to somebody, who then has to bear his or her testimony and toss the bear on to somebody else.

"I think Lorraine has something very special to talk about today," Sister Clifford said.

Even the leaders had heard.

I hugged the teddy bear. Its furry body reminded me of my moose slippers.

"It's too special for me to talk about," I murmured.

Sister Clifford looked at me curiously, but then she said, "OK. We understand. Toss the bear to somebody else, if you'd like."

I threw it to Blairsden Comisky because I knew he would say something funny and make people laugh. Then maybe they'd forget about my red convertible. My *phantom* red convertible. And my *phantom* dad.

Only he wasn't a phantom. He was real. He'd sent me the slippers, hadn't he? He'd send me a letter soon.

Even Blairsden couldn't make everybody forget, and the last thing Ardean said to me as we left was, "Tell your dad to tell my dad about that convertible."

As Thelma drove us home in her cranky old brown Plymouth, I had the dumb thought that if my dad had enough money to buy me a red convertible, what he should really do was get Thelma something that wasn't so close to collapsing.

For just a second I felt noble about giving up the convertible.

I had to be really around the bend, thinking that way.

"Help me, Dad," I whispered silently.

Philip Atterbury was slumped down in his seat, which wasn't like him at all. Generally he was making comments about things along the way.

I turned to look at him. "What's up, Doc?"

"Nuthin'." The word came out like a sigh.

I turned all the way around to face him. "This is Phoenix speaking," I said. "You can tell me."

His face brightened. "FEEEEN-ix," he said. "*That's* what it is."

I was puzzled. "What *what* is?"

He ducked his head. "In sharing time I told everybody there was a place called KLEEEN-ex, Arizona. They all laughed at me."

"Naw," I said. "They laughed *with* you. They thought you were making a joke."

Philip Atterbury thought about it. "Really?"

"Really," I said. "It's a pretty good joke."

Philip Atterbury looked out of the car window. He smiled suddenly and waved. "That's David Davenport," he said. "His dad says I can come with them to the fathers and sons campout. Did you know David has seven warts on his big toe? It looks like a pickle."

He giggled.

Philip Atterbury was back to normal.

Thelma glanced at me. "Thanks," she said.

She looked at the street again. "This is Thelma speaking," she said. "You can tell me."

She knew.

Of course she did. If everybody else at church had heard, so had she.

I sat silently for two blocks. Then I said, "Bob's a pencil. They're all going to laugh at me."

She caught on. "Maybe they'll think it's a pretty good joke."

"Maybe they won't."

"We'll be here for you, hon," Thelma said. "Philip Atterbury and I."

I knew they would be.

No matter what happened, Thelma and Philip Atterbury would still love me and try to make me laugh and put their arms around me.

Not my dad. Maybe he'd never be there to help me.

Maybe all I would ever get from him was moose slippers and an occasional Christmas card.

So OK. Didn't I have a family already? Not the dad-and-mom-and-kids kind that Thelma talked about, the kind that they showed pictures of in Primary.

But not *everybody* had that kind anyway.

The first thing I did when we got home was get my moose slippers and put them on Thelma's feet.

"You don't need Howard," I said. "You've got these to keep you warm."

"You're a nut, hon," she said. But she laughed, and so did Philip Atterbury.

The second thing I did was pull the pencil named Bob from my backpack. I erased *Phoenix* from the top of my notebook and very firmly wrote *Lorraine*.

It was the only true me who would face my friends and tell them they might have to be satisfied to ride in a cranky old brown Plymouth when I turned sixteen.

The third thing I did was get my Families Are Forever poster and hang it over the kitchen table where we played Chutes and Ladders for family home evening.

Lael Littke is a full-time writer who lives in Pasadena, California, with six cats and two dogs. She has one married daughter who also lives in California. She is the author of more than thirty books for teenagers and younger readers, and has published books in the LDS and national markets. Her most recent books include the *Bee There* series for LDS readers and *What about Lenore?* Though she now spends most of her time writing books, she began her fiction writing career by writing short stories and enjoys the chance to create stories like "A Pencil Named Bob" whenever she has the chance.

What might be the most difficult thing for a kid to endure? Alienation at school?
The loss of a dear friend? Failure in the things they most hope for?
How about the loss of a father?

A Harbor of My Own

Carol Lynch Williams

IT WAS THE DAY MY FATHER DIED that I found the Church.

Wait, I guess I should back up and tell you that my dad is still alive and that I've always been a member.

But it was the day he died that I found the Church.

I had come down to breakfast, and there was Mom, sitting at the counter. She still held the phone in one hand as if it were precious to her. In her other hand she held a mug of orange juice. Her pink terry-cloth bathrobe was opened slightly, and I could see the crisp line of her pajamas, pink too, peeking out. Pajamas make me uncomfortable. Too-big T-shirts are the way to go for me.

"He's having an affair," she said the moment I came in. Just like that, no warning—unless you count the phone sitting in her hand as a warning. I mean, how many people hold onto a phone for no reason, except maybe for dear life?

"Who is?" I said, but I knew. I think it was the phone that gave it away.

"Something's happened to him. He's changed. I saw it coming, but I didn't believe it. He's probably sitting on an Australian beach with her right this very minute."

"I don't think so," I said, sure then she was talking about Dad. "There's a big time difference between here and there. It's late at night for him. And cold, too. They're in the middle of their winter."

Mom pressed her lips to the back of the phone like she was kissing it good-bye, and I waited for permission to move on in life because my father, she said, was having an affair.

22

"Anyway, who could give up the beaches we have here? I mean, New Smyna's the World's Safest Beach—it says so on signs," I said. "Come on, Mom, would you choose an Australian beach over a Florida beach?"

"He just called, Annie," Mom said.

"What did he say?" I asked.

Mom took a deep breath and pushed at her light-colored bangs with the hand holding the juice. I watched the drink slip toward the lip of the cup and waited for it to spill out onto the counter, but it never did. "He's extending his trip. And when he comes home, he wants a divorce."

"Oh," I said. Mom's words had given me the permission I needed to begin to move around again, so I made myself a bowl of Wheat Chex cereal and somehow managed to swallow it, which isn't so easy when you're barely chewing. I've noticed that when your whole body has turned to ice, things don't hurt so much and you move a lot slower.

"I'm going," I said at last, putting the bowl into the sink. A pattern of small pastel flowers raced around the edge of the china that Dad had told Mom to go ahead and buy only a few weeks before.

Mom didn't look at me. In fact, when I left the room, left the house a few minutes later, she was still holding onto the phone, still waiting with her orange juice.

As soon as I stepped into the real morning outside, I felt like I watched my whole life from another person's eyes. It was as if the inside me was trapped in a bubble and the outside me was going along like nothing really horrible was happening with my dad.

"I'm going to see Vicki," I said to the sun and the hot wind and the grasses that stayed green no matter what the temperature. I was testing to see if my voice still worked. It did.

Vicki and I have been best friends since who knows when. She joined the Church a couple of years ago, but she's never been active.

It took me only a few minutes to get to Vicki's place, and I walked on in without knocking like I always do in the summer. Her parents work, and they're rarely home.

"Hey," I called. "I'm here."

The cream-colored tile under my feet felt especially cool, maybe because the day was starting to get hot or maybe because I was worried about my father. *No, wait, that doesn't make sense,* I thought. And then, *How could you, Dad?*

I padded down the carpeted hall to Vicki's room and pushed open her door. She was still in bed.

"Get up," I said. "It's almost noon." That wasn't quite the truth. It was just after nine.

Vicki didn't move. She played her part perfectly, doing the same thing she did every morning.

"Come on," I said. "The day's a-wasting." I would have opened the blinds like I always did when I came to get Vicki out of bed, but they were already open and light poured in. It was so pure-looking, that light, it hurt. I felt a stab of pain in my chest.

I pulled the pillow from Vicki's head and waited for her to tell me to get out.

"Get out," she said, her face down in the mattress.

That's good, I thought. *Things are normal here. Maybe Mom made a mistake. Maybe Dad—*

"Get outta here. The sun's barely up." Vicki's voice was rough with sleep.

And then, maybe because I wasn't the one feeling normal, I left.

I went back home as fast as I could without running. My head seemed to be attached to my body with a balloon string, and it bounced along, jumbling my mind and thoughts.

"Mom's wrong," I said at last. "She's made a terrible mistake." By then I was home.

Mom wasn't at the counter anymore, and the phone had been hung up.

The phone again.

I did then what I thought I would never do, partially because things had changed so much in such a short amount of time: I called Dad.

"Country Comfort, Melbourne," the hotel operator said. Her accent was rich and sweet-sounding to me.

"Room 404," I said.

"Do you realize that it's three in the morning here?"

I hesitated a moment. Three in the morning. I'd be waking him up. I took a breath. "I know the time," I said. My heart started pounding.

"I'll connect," the voice said.

The phone began ringing double rings. After a moment my father picked up. "Hello?" I swallowed at the lump that filled my throat from hearing his voice. My mouth wouldn't work. I squeezed my eyes shut.

"Hello?" he said again, his voice just as groggy as before.

"Daddy?"

"Oh, Annie," he said, and he no longer sounded sleepy. "How are you, honey?"

My heart slowed a bit. This was my father I was talking to. He sounded the same as he always did. Mom *must* have made a mistake.

"I'm doing OK," I said. "How are you?"

Dad laughed a little. "Tired. I think you caught me right in the thick of REM sleep."

"Oh," I said. "Sorry." How could I tell my father what my mother had said? Silence passed between Dad and me.

"What is it, Annie?" Dad said. "Have you spoken to your mother? Has she told you something we need to talk about?"

Oh no. It was true. Everything was true.

"Well, yeah," I said. "She's told me some stuff, but I couldn't really believe it."

"Annie," Dad said. And right then, right with that word, with my name Annie, I felt the change in him. The one Mom had talked about. "I'm not coming home for a while after all. I've decided to stay. Collect myself. See what's right for me."

I felt the blood drain from my face, starting at the roots of my hair. It took its time leaving and left me chilled, except for the hand that held onto the phone. That hand was warm. Maybe all my blood had gone there.

"What do you mean, what's right for you?" I said. "Aren't Mom and I right for you?" My heart was pounding again. I was either burning a lot of fat calories or getting ready to have a heart attack. I wasn't sure which I wanted to have happen.

"You'll always be right for me, honey," Dad said. "You're my daughter. But . . ."

I didn't say anything.

"But not everything that I have in my life now is right for me."

I still didn't say anything.

"Your mom and I haven't gotten along since I started this traveling. I need my freedom, you know. Things aren't real good with her. I'm sure she told you."

"She said you're having an affair," I said, pushing the words out of my mouth with a shove from my tongue. The blood rushed back to my face. How could I say such an awful thing to him, to my own father? I was so embarrassed I was glad that thousands of miles separated us.

"No, Annie, I'm not having an affair. But I have met someone else."

"Dad," I said.

"I know it hurts you. But I'm not doing anything wrong. Not really."

"You're already married," I said. "Meeting someone new seems wrong to me. What about the Church? What about the things we believe?"

Dad was quiet a moment. "I've decided those things aren't for me. I don't need the crutch of a religion. I've learned that being out here and away from your mom. Alicia has helped me to see that, too."

"Alicia?" I said.

"My friend," Dad said. "But I started noticing even before she and I met. The Church just isn't right for me. It's too confining. I can't do all I want."

"What is it you want?" I asked. "I don't get it, Dad. You're the one who's always telling me that the gospel is a harbor in the storm."

"Not for a while I haven't," Dad said. And I remembered with a jolt that it was true. "But my life's not so turbulent anymore. I don't need organized religion. Make sure you need the Church, Annie."

"I do need it," I said. "I'm hanging up, Dad. Go back to sleep. Get back into your REM stuff."

"Now, Annie," Dad said. "Don't be angry with me. I'm happy with what I've chosen."

"Are you?" I asked. "Well, I'm not. Good-bye."

And I hung up the phone. That's when my dad died. Right at that moment. He was changed to me. His voice had proven it. So had his words.

I closed my eyes and kept my hand on the receiver.

"Well?" Mom asked.

I looked over at her, surprised she was in the room. When had she come in? "He's not coming back any time soon," I said.

Mom nodded. I could tell from where I sat that she had been crying. Her eyes and nose were red.

She smiled at me. "There's still you and me," she said.

I couldn't say anything. Those words weren't what I wanted to hear.

"And we'll make it through. It's terrible, but we'll make it."

"Not me," I said. "This is the worst thing that's ever happened to me. And I don't see how you can even say we. Not with Dad gone."

A look of pain crossed Mom's face, but I ignored it.

"Oh, Annie," she said.

And then I ran out of the room, out of the house, and back into the bubble that seemed to keep me separated from the world.

I'd like to say that once I was able to get down to the beach, the bubble popped and everything straightened itself out. But that's not true. In fact, the whole time I walked it seemed my feet slapped out a tuneless song that my mind fit words to. *He's not coming back; he doesn't believe. He's not coming back; he doesn't believe. He's not coming back; he doesn't believe* went though my mind so much I thought I'd stop right there on the sandy path and start to bawl.

"Stop it," I said aloud to my mind. "Let me alone."

But the chant didn't quit.

On the World's Safest Beach that day, the words stayed in the back of my mind. And a few more came to pick at me. I remembered

Dad saying that he didn't need organized religion anymore. And then his warning, "Make sure that you need the Church, Annie."

I sat on the beach up close to the dunes and thought of the gospel and its place in my life. I thought of my dad giving me blessings and, before now, always being there. What had changed him? Would it happen to me?

The sun began to set, painting the thin clouds bright pink and orange. An ache bigger than the ocean, it seemed, flooded my guts, and I felt like I was drowning in it. *Make sure that you need the Church, Annie* went through my head again and again.

Did I need the gospel? Did I need God? I left the beach without answers. It was way past dinnertime when I got home. I was starving from the day, exhausted because of my father. And I found Mom and Vicki waiting for me in the kitchen.

"Where have you been?" Vicki asked.

"Thinking." I could tell by looking at them that they had been talking about Dad. "What did you decide?"

"What do you mean?" Vicki said.

Mom moved, nervous, and began wiping the already clean counter.

"About my dad," I said. "What did you decide about my dad?"

Vicki's dark-brown eyes grew a bit wider. "We didn't decide anything about him. We were waiting for you."

I took a deep breath and let the air out of my lungs. "And what did you decide about me?"

"That we love you, Annie," Mom said.

I looked at my mother and my friend, and right then the bubble began to get thinner. I know it sounds crazy, but it's true. Knowing somebody cared made my heart not feel so pained. "Thanks," I said.

In bed that night, my long T-shirt cool against my skin at least for the moment, I thought about Dad. I remembered the first time he left to travel overseas. He'd given both Mom and me a blessing. I saw him for a moment as if he were standing in my room. I could almost feel the pressure of his hands on my head, almost smell his aftershave. And in my memory I felt the power of the priesthood and that blessing as if it were happening to me all over again.

I began to cry. "Daddy," I said. "Daddy." My whole self ached at the possible loss of my father and his priesthood.

I crawled out of bed and knelt on the floor. I clinched my hands together and squeezed my eyes shut. And I prayed, because I knew now that I did need religion. I did need the gospel of Jesus Christ. I did need God. My memory had told me so.

There was no burning bush for me, and no angel came to visit. But a simple, easy restfulness entered my heart, calming me in the very places I had hurt so deeply before. The bubble was gone.

At last I got up. I made my way out into the hall and down to my parents' room. Mom's door stood open wide. A bit of moon-light came in through her window, and I could just see her lying in her bed, under the mauve sheets.

"Mom," I said, hoping I would and would not wake her.

She sat right up. "What is it, Annie?"

I cleared my throat. "I wanted you to know that I think the two of us are gonna make it through this. We've got each other." I reached out, and my hand touched the jamb of the door. The wood was smooth beneath my fingers.

Mom opened her arms to me, and I went over close to hug her.

Carol Lynch Williams is the mother of five daughters and has been married for almost thirteen years to Drew Williams, who is also a writer. She is the author of several books, including *Kelly and Me* (1993), *Adeline Street* (1995), *The True Colors of Caitlynne Jackson* (1997), and *If I Forget, You Remember* (1998). Her next book, *My Angelica,* will be published on Valentine's Day, 1999. She has also co-written the Latter-day Daughter Series with Launi K. Anderson. A convert to the Church, she served an LDS mission to North Carolina where she worked with deaf people.

two

Fathers
Relationships
Testimony
Decisions

Talk about social claustrophobia:
Jeff is stuck riding with a cocky oddball for 848 miles.
Can Jeff survive?
Will Carlton?

ACROSS THE PLAINS WITH CARLTON THRASHBERRY

Donald Smurthwaite

Mile Zero

IT IS 4:45 A.M., MORE THAN AN HOUR before daylight. The headlights of Carlton Thrashberry's car are shining in the driveway and he has already honked the horn twice. I see the lights in the Palfreymans' home across the street turning on and wonder if a call is being made to the police.

Carlton bounds out of his car and raps on our door. I open it, and he steps into our entry. Carlton is dressed in long plaid shorts and a T-shirt that shows a polar bear with sunglasses sitting under an umbrella sipping a tall, cool drink. Under the polar bear are the words, *Keep your cool, dude.*

"Hey, Big J, my main man of the day, just the two of us, ready to attack the road in my machine, all the way from here to Provo. You ready? My engine is running, and I'm not talking about the car!"

My mom sleepily wanders around the corner from the living room and gives me a kiss. "Good-bye, Jeff. Call us when you get there." My dad comes out in his bathrobe, rubbing his whiskers, yawning. He shakes hands with me, wishes me luck, and tells us to drive safely. They smile numbly, propped on each other, as I load my suitcases in the car while Carlton gives me directions on what I should put where. I wave farewell to my parents, and Carlton throws his car into reverse and we are off.

"Nice touch, Big J, the little scene at the door with Mom and Pop. But now for the big-time adventure: Miles of open highway calling our names, two dudes on their way up and out. Do ya know what I mean?"

Carlton really talks like this. I wish I were kidding, but I am not. I am going to be with Carlton for approximately the next fifteen hours of my life as we make our way back to BYU from Portland.

It promises to be a very long day.

Mile 27

Carlton has talked nonstop for the first half-hour of our trip. The most I have managed to work in is two "Uh-huhs" and one "Wow." We are not even to Hood River yet, and he has already told me of his plan that will rescue the federal government from the national deficit, who will win the World Series, and why *Moby Dick* should not be considered the Great American Novel. It is difficult to tell what is running faster at this point, the car engine or Carlton's mouth.

I look over at him as his mouth motors on. Carlton is not very tall and has kind of a big nose. His black hair is cut short. My guess is that it's the same hairstyle he's worn for the last twenty years. He moved into my ward just before I went on a mission and just after he returned from his. We're not exactly close friends. In fact, he would not make my list of my favorite thousand people. Frankly, I try to avoid him as much as possible because he talks so much.

We're making this trip together because I don't have a car yet and I need to be back in Provo early to look for a job. Carlton was the only person who was leaving two weeks before classes started, although his motive was less practical than mine. "You get there first, it gives you an advantage with the women," he told me. "You get to meet them before any other guys. They think of guys, and you're the first one to pop into their memory banks. First is first and last is last. Do ya know what I mean?"

I told him not really.

"Big guy, you are sweet but you are a project and I have only another fourteen hours to raise the quality of your life by mountainous proportions."

Fourteen hours. I wish he hadn't reminded me.

Mile 69

We are on a really pretty stretch of the interstate, a portion that up until now I had always enjoyed driving. Carlton is giving me a geology lecture concerning the basalt flows in the Columbia River Gorge. I manage another "Uh-huh" and break into new territory with a "Really?" over the next five minutes.

Carlton suddenly stops talking and looks over at me. "Big J, you're a nice guy but not much at the fine art of conversation. You got to open up, man. You've got to get *in touch*."

"I'll try, Carlton," I utter, my first complete sentence in more than an hour.

He smiles again and continues jabbering. We have approximately 750 miles to go.

Mile 94

Carlton's car has only an AM radio. Please understand, I am not the kind of guy who needs a million-dollar car stereo system that shakes the foundations of tall buildings when the bass is cranked up. But a good radio or cassette deck would have been welcome—no, make that *critical* to preserve my mental health. We're losing the signal of the only station his ancient radio can pull in, and that makes for a very bizarre situation.

Carlton, you see, has begun singing rap.

He sort of makes *bukka chenk, bukka chenk, bukka chenk, chenk, chenk* noises.

"This might surprise you, dude, me doing rap. A lot of people don't really think of it as music, if ya know what I mean. But I do. I'm into rap. Big time. Actually, rap reminds me of some of the early, primitive blues, which as everybody knows is the foundation of modern rock."

I figure the next major town with a radio station is Pendleton, and it is still one hundred miles away. Until then, we'll just rap our merry little way down the road.

Bukka chenk, bukka chenk, bukka chenk, chenk, chenk.

Mile 246

We are driving in the Blue Mountains of eastern Oregon. I won't say that Carlton rapped the whole last 120 miles. But I'd bet my prize 1956 Mickey Mantle baseball card that he sang rap for at least ninety of them. Where did he learn that stuff? We did pick up a cowboy-music station for a while, and yippie-yo-ki-yay never sounded so good. Now I am again growing nervous because we're losing the station to static. Is more rap in store?

Carlton reaches over and turns off the radio. I brace myself for more bukka chenks.

But I am pleasantly surprised. Carlton says he's about rapped out. "Let's talk," he suggests.

"Good. Talk. We can do that."

"Let's talk about clothes. Clothes make the man, you know."

My stomach knots up. I do not want to talk about clothes with Carlton Thrashberry. *Bukka chenk* would be welcome at this point.

"I'm not saying you're a dud, man, when it comes to sartorials, but you could use a little brotherly guidance. Clothes are an expression, a statement, and Big J, your duds say only one word about you: boring."

"I kind of like being boring, Carlton."

"I know, Big J, and that's where I'm going to help you."

For the next hour, he talks to me about his theory of clothes, which summarized is read your mood, dress accordingly, and don't worry about colors that clash. I nod occasionally and cut loose a few times with what has become my favorite expression on this trip: uh-huh. This segment of our journey concludes with an offer of help from Carlton. "Bud, my Big J, when you decide it's time to shed your cocoon and you want to become a beautiful yet macho butterfly, then you give your man Carlton a call and we'll do some shopping for threads together. It will be *el instant image changeo*. The ladies will go nuts. And your hair could use some work, too."

I thank him very much while trying to ignore the fact that the man who has offered to be my personal wardrobe consultant is wearing a T-shirt silk-screened with a polar bear reclining on a lounge chair.

Mile 311

In one of the rare moments when he is not talking, hoping to get into something at least a little meaningful I ask Carlton what he is majoring in.

"Public relations and advertising," he says. "I've got a natural feel for it. The old PR personality, good with people. That's yours truly. And what about you? How are you going to make your mils?"

"Journalism," I say weakly, bracing for what I know is coming.

"Radical! That means we're in the same college! Maybe we'll have some classes together. This is a news story, people!"

Suddenly, accounting is becoming a very attractive career.

Mile 388

We have crossed the state line and are now in Idaho. Apparently this simple feat of driving triggers some bittersweet memories for Carlton.

"Ah, Idaho. What could have been. A heart breaks," he says mysteriously.

I know I'm taking the bait, but I'm deathly afraid of more rap or another lecture on how I should dress or comb my hair. I grit my teeth.

"What do you mean, Carlton?"

"I dated the runner-up in the Miss Idaho contest last year," he says matter-of-factly. "Sweet kid. Nuts about me, too. She wanted to get married, but I told her I wasn't ready. I told her there was still too much for me to experience, that I wasn't ready to settle down and be a one-woman man. I didn't want to slip the old ring on the finger and tack my feet to the ground. She cried. Dude, how she cried. But she said, 'Carlton, I knew that about you. You're a wanderer and a rambler. But I'll always love you.' Broke her heart."

Carlton sighed. A long, *romantic* sigh. "A wanderer and a rambler. Crazy kid," he says, shaking his head.

I felt nauseated. Runner-up to Miss Idaho my foot. Unless females had changed a whole lot in the two years since my mission, Carlton had about as much chance with the Miss Idaho runner-up as I did of going to work next week as a political columnist for the *New York Times*.

We are almost halfway to Provo. *Halfway*. I wonder how much a bus ticket to Provo from Boise would cost. Is any cost too high to preserve my sanity?

Mile 443

Boise. Lunchtime. I suggest to Carlton that we pull off for a big, greasy hamburger and some french fries.

He looks appalled. "Have you ever been to a slaughterhouse? Do you know what goes on there? Man, it's bitter to the max."

We end up at a grocery store, spooning salad into plastic containers and drinking a bottle of guava juice.

Mile 492

We are on what is known as the Snake River Plain. I know that because Carlton told me that's what this place is called, just as he has pointed out every other major land form during the last nine hours. It's another chapter of our travelogue Carlton Thrashberry and me crossing the plains together.

There isn't a lot to do on this part of the drive, unless you are excited by brown, rolling mountains covered by brown, brittle grass. I know I shouldn't, I know it is not the right thing to do, but I can't help it. I begin to mentally list the things that annoy me about Carlton.

1. He talks too much.
2. When he talks, which is almost always, he almost always talks about himself.
3. Carlton thinks he is cool, and I think he is not.

4. I don't like his car. It's a squatty little compact with no guts that was mercifully taken off the production line by a major automaker about two years after its introduction. But Carlton calls it his Rolling Thunder and keeps telling me that it is the best thing ever to hit the highways of America.

5. Carlton knows everything, just ask him.

6. I don't like his voice, I don't like his nose, I don't like the way he parts his hair. I don't like his clothes, I don't like the way he sings rap, I don't like being called Big J, and I don't like his dietary habits, however healthy they may be.

7. And I don't think he ever dated the runner-up in the Miss Idaho contest.

Well, that about covers it.

Mile 664

For the last twenty miles, I have been nervous. I look over at the gas needle and it seems we are running on fumes. The last time we gassed up was in La Grande, Oregon. I question Carlton about the needle teetering on E.

"No problem. Me and the Rolling Thunder are so in tune with each other that I can tell you within two miles of when she'll run out of gas. Perfect harmony between a man and his machine. We'll make Snowville easy, and we could probably cruise all the way into Tremonton. Do ya know what I mean?"

Seven minutes later, Rolling Thunder coughs, sputters, and dies.

"Hmmm. Must be out of gas," Carlton shrewdly observes.

I begin to think how nice it would feel to wrap my fingers around his scrawny, little neck and shake his pointy, little head just to where his eyes start to bug out even more than they naturally do.

"Hey, something sweet may come of this, Big J. Maybe some really fine-looking ladies bound for school will come along and give us a ride to Snowville. Maybe we'll marry one of them. Awesome, dude!"

"Carlton," I say in a surprisingly calm voice that masks the volcanic eruption rumbling just below skin surface. "You stay here. Do not leave the car. I will walk into Snowville and get a can of gas. I repeat, do not leave the car. And after I get the can of gas, I might—just might—come back here with it. It is your only chance."

Carlton looks bewildered. "Hey, don't go away mad."

I begin tromping down the freeway. He calls out to me, "At least you're coming out of your shell a little, Big J!"

It is approximately ninety-seven degrees, the wind is blowing grit in my eyes, and I am not happy. As I get about a hundred yards down the road, I look back. Carlton has his sunglasses on and is slouched against the side of his car. He seems to be talking to himself. Perhaps it is an expression of remorse for being so infernally dumb. Perhaps there is hope for Carlton. The wind blows my way and I pick up a bit of his conversation with himself.

I'm the berry man and there's nothin' in my tank, bukka chenk, bukka chenk, bukka chenk, chenk, chenk. . . .

Mile 802

The lights of Salt Lake City are to my left. The unplanned stop in the desert for gas cost us two hours, and the sun has just set. This has been a long, horrible day. The end, though, is almost in sight. I will never again drive anywhere with Carlton Thrashberry.

I am leaning over, holding my head in my hands.

"Not feeling well, Big J?"

"I have a headache, Carlton. Do not bother me."

"Oh, I've got it," he says smugly. "You're worried about the big M."

"The what?"

"The big M. Finding your EP. Marriage and your eternal partner. Look, I've been there. Fresh off your mission, and you know that the next female you see on campus may be Miss Right for you. Pressure, whoa. You'd better believe it. Now, if you're worried about dating or any other aspect of the courting game, you just check in with me and I'll steer you right. Promise. I know what you're feeling, bud."

"Carlton, trust me on this one. You do not know what I am feeling. You do not want to know."

"OK, but the offer is still good."

I put my head down again and cannot help groaning.

Mile 848

We are in Provo. I want to kiss the ground. Our trip is over. I have survived with most of my senses intact. I have survived Carlton, therefore I can survive anything that school dishes out.

Carlton pulls into the parking lot of his apartment. He wants me to help unload his belongings. He wants to check in with his new roommates and then get me settled in my apartment.

"Always an adventure, meeting roommates," he says. "Funny, I never seem to keep the same ones for very long. But it fits my style just fine."

We trudge upstairs to his apartment. Most people would knock, but this is Carlton and he is not most people. He throws open the door and takes two steps in. Three people are in the living room watching television. One guy looks like he should be on a surfboard: tall, sandy brown hair, drop-dead good looks. The other fellow is as big as a tight end, and it's a cinch he's never had to worry about a date on the weekend.

The third person is a visiting girl, and she—oh, she merely looks like she just stepped off a modeling set in New York City. I'm getting an inferiority complex and I'm just *visiting*. They all turn and stare at Carlton and his polar bear T-shirt.

His confidence flutters. He smiles limply. "Carlton Thrashberry here, and the runner-up in the Miss Idaho pageant wants to marry me!"

The model yawns, turns to her friends, and says, "Who let him in?"

The journey is over. My suitcases and boxes are all in place at my apartment.

Carlton has been fairly quiet since we finished up at his apartment. I walk back with him to Rolling Thunder. He looks up at me. "Thanks for coming along. Sometimes I wonder if I get on people's nerves because of my high energy output."

"Don't worry, Carlton. Thanks for the lift. I've got to call my folks now. You know how parents are. They worry about you all the time."

Carlton looks at the curb. He thrusts his hands deep into his pockets and looks puzzled and worried.

"Jeff, am I—well, am I OK?"

Carlton Thrashberry, you are all mine.

This is the moment I've dreamed about since 4:45 A.M. Revenge. For 848 miles I've been thinking of all the things I'd like to tell him: Carlton, you are obnoxious, you are self-centered, you are a crummy dresser, and you can't sing rap worth beans. A feeling of power surges through me.

And then I flip the switch, click it all off. This isn't right.

"Yes, Carlton. You are an OK guy. You have a lot going for you."

He looks relieved. Above his big nose, his eyes shine happily in the glow of the parking lot light. "See ya round then, bud. Take care."

"You too, Carlton. Take care."

It has been two years since I've seen Carlton. He graduated and then moved to Texas, or so I heard. It's funny that I even think of him, but I do now and then. And when I think of him, I have good thoughts. I can't explain why, unless maybe that I'm wiser now than when we drove across the plains together.

I'd like to see him again. I'd like to say to him, "Carlton, I hope you're having a good life. I hope you've got a good job and work with nice people who like you. I hope you and the runner-up worked things out, and that you're happily married, and that your first baby is on the way. I hope she's a girl and that she looks just like her mom. I hope you've given up singing rap and have a decent car, and that you're doing well in PR. Carlton, I wish the best for you."

Yeah, that's what I'd say to him.

It's crazy, but it's the right thing for me to think about Carlton and everybody else in this world like him.

Do you know what I mean?

Donald Smurthwaite was born in Portland, Oregon, and now lives in Boise, Idaho. Both of his novels, *The Search for Wallace Whipple* and *Do You Like Me, Julie Sloan?* are set in western Oregon. He has written dozens of magazine stories, both fiction and nonfiction. He got the idea for "Across the Plains with Carlton Thrashberry" while driving home from a vacation where things didn't work out the way he had planned. He and his wife, Shannon, are the parents of four children. He's served in a variety of church positions, and currently is bishop. Donald is at work on a third novel, which he hopes to finish sometime before the end of the century.

SOLO

Kristen Randle

I SUPPOSE THAT THE END OF YOUR SENIOR year is a natural time for epiphanies—the last football game, the last Christmas dance, the last everything. I ate lunch on the lawn Wednesday, just messing around with my friends—you can't believe how funny these guys are. Anyway, I was just sitting there, looking around, listening to some story of Joel's, and I saw this bunch of sophomores sitting together. These were kids I knew—some were in the band, some were in seminary—and suddenly, it hit me; next year at this time, they know where they'll be—they'll still be there sitting here on this lawn in the sun, messing around with basically the same friends they have now. But I won't be here. I'll be gone. Me and these friends of mine, all of us—way gone.

I couldn't eat the rest of my lunch after that. It's not that I want things to stay the same; I can't wait to be out of this school. But I'm going to miss Joel and Alicia and Matt and Joce, this sitting here.

I've been lucky. I've always had the same house, the same yard, the same friends; the word *home* is deep in me. But I should have known this was coming. I'm the youngest kid in my family—I've been watching it all unravel for years; first my brother, gone to France on a mission. Then my sister decided to go to UCLA. One by one, they've gone. At first, it was cool—I mean, I finally got my own room, and nobody was beating on me. But then it seemed weird, especially that first Christmas without Nick.

44

I could see how hard it was on my mom; I mean, she was glad that he went on the mission, and all. But still—it made things feel so different, emptier, and it was only the beginning.

And all of this's been going through my head tonight—tonight's my last jazz band concert. We decided to wear concert black, even though it's jazz, because it's the last one for me and Ryan and Allen and Amy. I was getting dressed, all the time thinking about my parents—about how cool they are—about how they've always come to everybody's everything—every game, every National Honor Society induction, every play, every concert.

But this is, like, *it*. The last thing. The last moment of the last kid.

This is the end.

I had to go early to set up. Which meant I wasn't home for dinner. Not that that's new. But it hurt me, somehow—thinking about my parents sitting at the table all alone. That table used to be a wild place when the six of us were all crowded around it. Some of the guys in the band were talking about going out to eat something after the concert tonight, but I was kind of reluctant to do that, thinking I better go home with my folks. My heart was really kind of hurting me, thinking about sending them home alone.

Anyway, we met early in the band room, then we set up on the stage in the commons. The janitors had already put the chairs out for the audience, but we had to do our own. I was busy lugging up the music stands, trying to keep track of the music. That's what we're going to be doing the whole last week of school—trying to put the music back together—who knows where some of these parts have ended up—so we can file it all away for somebody else to use after we're gone.

Now it's just before 7:00, and people are starting to file in.

I'm a little nervous; it's not like I haven't played tons of solos before. But this one—the one I'm going to play tonight—was different. I've really worked on this, put every bit of music I have into it; I'd used it as my audition piece for the university, and it got me a scholarship. And this is the last time I'm ever going to play it with this band. The last time I'm going to be playing on this stage.

My parents just got here. They're actually kind of dressed up, making an occasion out of it. My mom waves at me with the hand that isn't holding the coat and the program, and they find seats near the aisle, so I can see them while I'm playing. That's something else I like about them; they understand about stuff like that.

It makes a difference when you're doing something, playing on a team or something, to know that your own people care about how you're doing. I mean, really, it would probably be okay if they didn't come to stuff, as long as I could go home and tell them about it afterwards. But then, if I happen to do something that's really amazingly good—or if I crash—it'd be better not to have to just describe it to somebody. It's the sharing that's so cool, to have somebody else bragging about how great it was or griping about the ref or whatever.

And they've been doing this for a long time; Nick's over ten years older than I am. He was on teams and in the band—in a garage band, even—and all us other kids have done *something* that needed an audience. And my parents were always there, watching. I know because they dragged me to all Nicky's things and all Charlotte's and all Jack's. Something at least once a week, every week for the last twenty-seven years.

It's become, like, their whole life.

So I'm sitting here on the stage, sucking on my reed, trying not to get smacked by somebody's stand or slide or something while the band's settling down. And watching my parents, worrying about them.

Okay, this concert is going to be hard on me emotionally. But what is it going to do to them? Their last kid. The last thing I'll ever do in high school. What are they going to do after this? How are they going to live in that empty house?

My mom is going to cry tonight, no question.

The room is full of noise—a lot of people are here for this, talking and rustling around and finding chairs.

Ms. Harrington picks up the mike, and starts in on the welcome stuff. Now, it's getting quiet. Vaughn jabs me with his elbow and gives me this weird look, sucking on his mouthpiece so that his eyes look like slits. The audience is clapping. I'm laughing at Vaughn as Mr. Bacon comes out and takes a little bow. My stomach tightens up, and I get a little chill.

Mr. Bacon steps up on the box and looks at us. I really can't think about it, looking at him like this for the last time. So I fix on that baton like it controls the fate of the universe. He brings it up and we all tense, and then he beats it out, and the brass come blasting out like a wall of sound. I find myself thinking, *what are they going to do without Allen next year, because there's, like, nobody who can handle the bass trombone like that.*

We do "My Funny Valentine," and Ryan gets up and does his thing in it—he handles it really well. And then we do our section feature in "Groovin' Hard." We have a good bari sax who's only a sophomore, which is incredible. Vaughn's a junior, so he'll be first alto sax in the fall when I'm gone. But Amy's the only tenor and I think she's quitting. They're going to have some work to do, getting this band up to speed next year.

This whole thing is going by too fast. These songs are flowing past and through me and I can't seem to hold the moment at all. And the next one up's "Home Again." My song. My solo.

We shift around in our chairs, tug the music into place, look up. I am incredibly nervous. Mr. Bacon counts us off, and Marilyn starts in on the piano riff, which leads the percussion. This is a long song, with a lot of really good sections in it. We play through the brass feature and go into the keyboard solo. My heart's pounding and my hands are, like, totally shaking. Which is stupid; I've done this a million times. But every time, I'm afraid I'm going to knock the stand over when I get up, or at least dump the music, or trip over the chair, trying to get out front in time.

I glance at my parents.

But they aren't watching me.

Instead, they're looking at each other. My dad says something, and my mother's eyebrows go up and then she laughs.

The percussion section's almost over.

She laughs again. I keep glancing at them, trying to watch the music at the same time. She says something to him—he tries to take her hand and she smacks him one. And here I am, sitting up on the stage in front of all these people, just about to play the most important thing I've ever played in my life.

Mr. Bacon's looking at me. I gasp and get this surge of nerves and grab my music. I make it past the stand—Vaughn catches it as I go by—and I set the music on the stand in front of the band just as they play my lead-in.

I grab my reed and look down.

My folks are finally watching me. And I play that solo like I've never played anything in my life. Everything I have goes into it—everything I've ever had. The whole time, they're holding hands, smiling up at me.

And that's when I have my epiphany: my folks are here for my sake, not for theirs.

There's a lot of applause for me after I finish, some whistling and yelling, which should feel really good. But I have to climb back into my chair and finish the piece with my section.

When I glance up, I see that my mother is crying, just the way she's supposed to. Sort of the way she's supposed to. Which makes me feel a little better. Because the thing is, that little moment of clear vision has shaken me a little.

We have one more thing to play, "Not Really the Blues." We do it very well—people look like they want to dance in the aisles. My parents are beaming. And then it's over. People stand to applaud. Mr. Bacon steps off the box and takes a bow, and then he waves to us and we all stand up, bumping stands, dumping music, and we sort of incline our heads, laughing. Well, some of us are laughing; I find that I'm blinking a lot. They clap for a long time, and then they sort of peter out, and we're still standing up there on the stage, looking around at the mess we've got to clean up.

I sit down in my chair. People in the audience are beginning to mill around. People up here on the stage are doing the same. But I'm thinking about this.

Maybe, all these years, my parents didn't even *want* to come to this stuff. Maybe they're *glad* this is the last one. But I don't like this thought. Maybe the truth's in the middle somewhere. But the fact of the matter is, whatever was going on between them down there in the audience, it could have been going on anywhere. And it probably would have been better if they'd been alone. Which means . . . which means that, even though they love me—even though they've loved all of us—they could be perfectly happy, just the two of them together. Alone. Without any kids.

Maybe they're looking forward to that, even.

Now, my parents are schmoozing around, talking to the other parents, thanking Mr. Bacon. I go down for a minute and stand beside them, smiling at people, accepting compliments. But after a while, I go back up on the stage and start cleaning up. My mom eventually finds me there and helps me stack music stands. She tells me how proud she is, and I can tell she means it. She gets teary-eyed again, which is not good for me, because my eyes want to answer. We finish the stands, and she and Dad offer to take me out for ice cream.

I think about it for a moment, feeling that old worry.

But finally, I tell them thanks, but the band's going out together, one last, loud, glorious, obnoxious time. And my folks grin at me, understanding.

I was pretty sure they wouldn't mind.

Kristen Randle has lived in many places in the United States from Los Angeles to Missouri to New York and Texas. She now lives in Utah. She has written six novels. Her fifth novel, *The Only Alien on the Planet,* has received an ALA Best Book award and was named the Michigan Library Association Book of the Year for 1996. She has also written short stories and songs and many other things. She believes there is nothing more glorious and painful than the period of life between childhood and grown-up-ness; the heart never quite gets over it. She sincerely hopes that you enjoy it while you have it.

*The first time Matt saw Camry, she was hanging upside down
from the branch of a tree on the bank of the Stone River.
She changed his life—and he helped change hers, too.*

BLUE LIKE A SALMON

Laura Torres

THE FIRST TIME I SAW CAMRY, she was hanging from the branch
of a tree on the bank of Stone River like an orangutan.

I tied a fly on the end of my leader in a hurry because I could
see the trout rising in the river and the sun was going down fast.

"Hey, you!" I heard. I looked around.

"Up here, in the tree!" She was in the branches above my
head, upside down. "Can you help me?" Her long, brown hair
hung straight down, and a wide smile lit up her freckled face.

"Uh, sure. Do you need help down?"

"No, but can I lower my line to you? It's taken me half an hour
to get it untangled from this tree," she said. "I can't figure out how
to get it and me down without one of us getting messed up."

I grabbed the line and lowered it carefully. The fly looked different than anything I'd seen. I found her rod by the trunk of the
tree. It was cheap, old, and beat up. I tried to reel in her line, but
I couldn't get it to work.

"It's broken," she said. She let her feet swing free, and she
dropped from the branch. "You have to kind of jury-rig it like this."

As she reeled in the line I noticed the scratches on her arms
from the branches. Her shirt sleeve was torn.

"You're bleeding," I said. She looked at her arm and shrugged
her shoulders.

"It was my very best fly. I couldn't leave it in the tree, and if the
leader broke off, well, then I'd be stuck because I don't have any
more. I'm Camry."

"Matt. Matt Sprague," I said.

"Thanks for your help," she said and walked to the river. Normally I'd be extremely annoyed if someone else was fishing my favorite hole, but I figured she wasn't the serious type, judging from her gear.

The fish were still rising, and I went back to tying my fly to the line. I heard a whoop coming from downstream. Camry was hauling in a good-size brown trout, a native, which were harder to catch than the stocked rainbows. I'd never caught one myself. I gave her a thumbs-up sign. It's unusual to see a girl on the river, let alone one catching browns on a dry fly.

"What are they biting on?" I hollered.

"The Camry Simmons Special," she hollered back.

"Sheez," I said and looked over my box of store-bought flies. None were anything like the one she was using. Another whoop. Another brown.

I tied on the closest thing I could find and cast a few times into a deep pool. Nothing. The sun was setting behind the mountain and the wind picked up, sending the trout deeper into the river. When I lost my fly on a log and snapped the line, I packed up my gear. I should have been annoyed, but instead I trudged up the side of the canyon behind her so I could see her. She cast her line a little differently than I'd been taught, but it made a satisfying swoosh in the air and the fly landed gracefully when she put it down. I watched her for a long time, until it got cold and dark, and left her there fishing by the moonlight with her broken rod, pulling in the elusive browns.

"Do you know a girl named Camry Simmons?" I asked Beth at lunch the next day. She knew practically everyone in our town, which made it all the more flattering she liked to hang out with me.

"Simmons. . . . No, I don't think so. Is she new?" Beth asked, picking at her salad.

"Yeah, but I haven't seen her at school," I said.

"Why are you so interested?" Beth asked, raising one eyebrow.

"No reason," I said, but I was already making plans to head straight for the river after football practice.

I cut out of practice early and made it to the river with an hour or so of sunlight left. When I got to my hole, the place I'd met Camry, I heard her voice. Three people were kneeling on the ground by the bank of the river. I slowed up and walked quietly. There was Camry and what I guessed were two sister missionaries, due to the way they were dressed. Even though I felt a little bad about eavesdropping, I listened to Camry pray.

"And please help me to be able to stay here in Utah for a long, long time, by this beautiful river and mountains and canyons. And please help my mom and Daryl come to their senses and let me be baptized," she said.

I couldn't make out the rest. When they'd said their amens and stood up, the missionaries' dresses were muddy at the hems and soaked through where they had knelt. They hugged Camry and walked up the canyon in their Sunday shoes to a waiting car. Camry stretched out on her back on the edge of the riverbank.

I waited a while so she wouldn't know I'd been listening, and then I walked downstream whistling like I didn't know she was sleeping there. I waded in the water and stood on a raised gravel bed where I was close enough to cast into a still pool.

"Ouch!" Something had hit the back of my head. I whirled around, and Camry was standing there pitching rocks at me.

"Get out of there, you idiot!" she shouted. "You're standing on a spawning bed!"

I looked at the clean gravel mounded around my boots. I should have known better.

"You didn't need to pelt me with those rocks," I said. Her ponytail was full of twigs and leaves, and her knees were muddy.

"I had to get your attention, didn't I?" she asked. "Whoa, that's a Winston, isn't it?"

I handed my rod over to her so she could look at it. I noticed she was wearing the same shirt she had on yesterday, the one with the rip in the sleeve.

"Would you like to try it?" I asked.

"No." She immediately handed it back. "It's yours."

She walked away, picked up her old rod from the riverbank, and began casting. I did the same, but after a while I felt awkward next to her obvious skill and ended up just watching her again. When she pulled in a brown, I caught it for her in my net and took the hook out of its mouth.

"When I was six, when I lived in Oregon, I went salmon fishing for the first time with my dad," she said as she released the brown. "I was scared to death of the first one I caught. It was so big and powerful. It flopped around on the ground so bad my dad finally hit it over the head with a rock. The funny thing was, I didn't know it was a salmon. I figured a salmon would be pink. I guess the only salmon I'd seen were the cut-up and skinned pieces in the grocery store. But it was blue, kind of silvery and iridescent. I still remember how beautiful it was and how smooth and cold it felt when I held it."

"So your dad is a fisherman," I said.

"My dad left me and my mom almost right after that trip, but I remember him saying, 'There's a fine line between fishing and standing on the shore like an idiot. Truest thing anyone ever did say.' I guess he made sure I wasn't one of the idiots before he left."

It was dark and I was late for dinner, so I reluctantly packed up my gear.

"Camry, do you live around here?" I asked.

"Yes," she said.

"I haven't seen you at school."

"I'm, uh, home schooled, I guess you could say." She looked real uncomfortable.

"Well, maybe I'll see you at church?" I asked.

"I'm not a Mormon," she said.

"But only because you're not baptized," I said. Then I realized I'd blown it. She stared at me for a long time. She didn't look mad, exactly, but definitely not thrilled I'd been eavesdropping.

"I'm not allowed to go to church," she finally said. "But I'll see you around." She started to walk off, but then stopped and turned. "Sorry about your head."

"She lives in a motel," Beth told me. We were trying to study for a trig exam.

"What?" I asked. My mind was on the river.

"I said, Camry Simmons lives in a motel. Her dad is some sort of a sales guy, and they're living at the Maple Leaf Motel on Center Street. They're not members of the Church. They've actually been here half a year, so they're not new, they just keep to themselves. That's everything I could find out."

I knew all this by now, but I didn't let on. I also knew that Camry's stepdad, Daryl, was involved in some shady pyramid-scheme sales thing involving eye cream that Camry said was really just Vaseline hand lotion funneled into tiny bottles with fancy labels. Camry said he wasn't smart enough to keep the scam going for very long and always got found out and that's why they had to move a lot, sometimes in the middle of the night. And I knew that her mom and Daryl didn't want her with the missionaries, so that's why she met with them at the river.

"I did ride by a few times and happen to see them getting into their truck," Beth said.

"I invited Camry to come to the youth activity on Tuesday," I told Beth, before she said any more.

"You did what?"

"I invited her to come to our activity on Tuesday. You know, the service project."

"If I hadn't seen her for myself, I'd think you were interested in her more than you're telling," Beth said.

"What's that supposed to mean?"

"She seems really different, Matt."

"She is," I said, and closed my trig book. "I've never met anyone like her."

On Tuesday evening, Camry showed up at my house early.

"I told Daryl I was going over to a friend's house whose mother might be interested in distributing eye cream," she said. She pressed a little bottle into my hand. "I feel bad telling a lie, so give this to your mother. But tell her it's hand lotion. Don't let her put it on her face."

I laughed and invited her in to sit down while I found my shoes. When I came back, I found her wandering around in the kitchen.

"This is a really great house, Matt," she said. "I mean, you can tell there's a lot of living going on here."

I picked up a few things off the floor, not noticing before what a mess it was. "Well, I have five younger brothers and sisters. When everyone is home you don't notice the mess, just all the kids running around."

Camry smiled. "I'd like to see that sometime," she said.

On the way over to the church, she talked fast and was really skittery.

"I've never been in the church before. It's funny how you can believe something with all your heart and soul and still feel scared to death to get close to it. Did I tell you I want to be baptized in Stone River? Don't you think that would be appropriate? Maybe by the spring Daryl and Mom will let me go to church for real, on Sundays, and maybe I can get baptized when the water warms up a little. Do you think the other kids will mind if I start coming on Tuesday nights? I should have worn something nicer."

"Camry, calm down," I said, although I did wonder what Beth would think of the flies that were hooked to the pocket of the same shirt she always wore, and of her hair, which was done up in pigtails. "Everything will work out, and you're going to be just fine."

We opened the church doors and ran into Beth, along with some of the other girls in her class.

"You must be Camry," Beth said with a warm smile. "We've been looking forward to meeting you." Camry glanced at me surprised, but I just shrugged my shoulders and breathed a huge sigh of relief as Beth hustled her off to meet everyone.

Camry worked harder than anyone packing the fruit baskets we were going to give to the older people in our town, and she chatted with some of the girls. I even saw her demonstrating her cast to a few of the guys with a yardstick and a ribbon.

Camry started coming to church every Tuesday night and seemed to get on all right with Beth and the others. One night the young men and women were split up. Beth said they were going to do something with hair and makeup while we played basketball.

During a break I went to get a drink of water and peeked into the room where Camry and Beth were.

I didn't see Camry, so I got Beth's attention and she came out in the hall with me.

"Where's Camry?" I asked.

"She left," said Beth. "Don't ask me why. All we were trying to do was do her a favor, but halfway into it she got all bent out of shape and left."

"What did you do?"

"It was nothing really. We were going to give her a makeover. You know, do her hair and nails, maybe a little makeup and some wardrobe advice. We were all there to learn. It's not like we tried to single her out, but somebody had to be the model." Beth looked close to tears. "We were just trying to help her, Matt, help her fit in, that's all."

I ran out of the building, jumped on my bike, and rode straight to the river, where I knew she'd be.

It was dark, but the moon was shining bright and I saw her almost immediately sprawled out on the riverbank like that day I saw her with the missionaries.

"Camry, it's freezing out here," I said. "Why are you sleeping?"

"I'm not sleeping," she said without opening her eyes. "I'm listening to the river."

I didn't know what else to do, so I laid down next to her. "Close your eyes and block out everything except the river. Let it fill up your whole head until there's nothing else," Camry said.

At first I just felt cold and uncomfortable, but after a while the sound of the water got louder and louder and blocked out the wind moving through the trees, the cars in the distance, and then even all my senses until there was only the river and Camry next to me.

I was startled when Camry sat up.

"That's something my dad taught me," she said. "He used to say if you focus on the river it gives you perspective."

"Camry, I'm sorry about what happened tonight. Beth and the others didn't mean to hurt your feelings."

"I know that," she said. "I'm not mad at them. I'm not mad at anyone." She took a Kleenex out of her pocket and wiped at her eyes, which had some sort of shimmery powder on them.

"It's just the way things have always been for me. I've never quite fit in anywhere after my dad left and Mom married Daryl and we started moving two or three times a year. I guess I thought it might be different here, with all of us believing the same. That's what I thought would make the difference." She tried to run her fingers through her hair, but it was sticky with hair spray.

"It will, Camry," I said, "but we just have to give it some time. We'll all get used to each other."

"When I'm with Daryl and my mom and have to keep everything I believe locked inside of me, I feel like I'm going to explode. But out here I can let it out, really feel my testimony, like it's filling up the river, the canyon, the whole sky. Nature can't keep you from God the way people can."

I leaned over and kissed her, surprising me as much as her. She hugged me tight, and a fly on her shirt pocket stabbed me in the chest. I jumped back and pulled the barb out.

"Oh, man, sorry!" Camry said, trying not to laugh.

"I think it's a Camry Simmons Special," I said. "Maybe this is good luck."

"Hang on a minute," she said and ran off. When she came back she had her rod.

"I keep it here so Mom doesn't have to see it. Says it reminds her of my dad." I tied on the fly, and Camry cast it. She was graceful and beautiful, as much in place here as the trees and rocks and moonlight shining on the river.

The splash of water from the fish taking the fly was followed by the sound of a horn blaring from the road. An old pickup was stopped on the road. The back was filled with mattresses and end tables, a couch and suitcases. The whole mess was held on with bungee cords and twine. Camry stepped into the river as the fish fought against the line. The pickup door slammed.

"Camry! Camry! You better be down here" a man shouted and then swore. "You better not try hidin', or I'm gonna whip your sorry—"

"Daryl!" a woman's voice yelled.

"Camry, is that Daryl and your mom?" I asked, panicked. She ignored the question, concentrating on her catch.

"I got it, Matt, come look," Camry said. She held the fish in her hands under the moonlight where I could see.

"It's a rainbow trout," I said.

"I knew it wasn't a native because it fought a little differently," she said. The fish flipped in her hands, but she held it gently, being careful of its gills.

"Camry! Where are you?" The voices alternated.

Camry stood there, calm as the moon's reflection on the water.

"It's really beautiful. Look at the coloring." She pointed to the spots on the fish's side.

"Camry, are you going to have to leave?" I asked. My throat was closing, and I was having a hard time breathing.

"It's silvery blue, don't you think?" she asked. "Blue like a salmon."

"We gotta be going, Camry!"

The trout was motionless in Camry's hands.

"I've kept it out too long," she said and ran to the water.

She held it in the river facing downstream, but it was motionless in her hands.

"Swim, fish. Please swim. Please be OK," she begged. She let it go to swim away, but it tipped and floated sideways. She started to cry.

"Hold it upstream," I said.

She turned the fish, and we watched as the water flowed around it, its gills expanding, moving, breathing. It became strong again and slapped her wrist with its tail as it sped away.

Camry ran up the bank and quickly gathered her things.

"Keep this stuff for me until I can come back," she said.

"When will that be? Where are you going?"

"I don't know. I don't know," she said.

"Maybe you can stay here. I'm sure we could arrange something. I could talk to the bishop. You could get baptized."

She shoved the rod into my chest and let go.

"I've wished those things so much it hurts," she said and ran toward her family. "But don't forget," she hollered over her shoulder, "I've got a date with Stone River."

I stayed for a long time after she left, my damp shirt near frozen on my back, her old broken rod in my hand, not knowing what to do. I thought about casting the rod, but I would have been clumsy compared to her grace. I thought about going back to the church to find Beth and the others. I thought about going home. In the end, I closed my eyes and let the sound of the river fill my head, the canyon, and the sky until there was nothing else.

Laura Torres is the award-winning author of ten books for young people. Her first four hands-on activity books have sold well over two million copies. She is also a newspaper journalist and frequent contributor to magazines. Fiction is her current passion, and she is working on a second young adult novel. Raised in the Pacific Northwest, Laura now resides in Mapleton, Utah, with her husband, John, and two children. In addition to writing, Laura enjoys quilting, the ocean, traveling, reading, and rainy weather.

Big sisters can make a big difference in your life.
When Amy's friendship with Adam gets too serious,
her older sister gives her some sound advice.

PETALS FOR AMY

Paul Pitts

LAST FRIDAY, AS THE SALESCLERK WAS carefully examining the
potted miniature rosebush, I felt a twinge of doubt. The boy was
only in high school like me. At least I'm a senior. He sighed and
studied the plant from a different angle.

As the bell on the door jingled, we both looked over. Adam
walked in. He located me and started walking over, his smile provid-
ing an extra dose of sunshine for every plant in Buds 'n' Blossoms.

"Hi," he said and let his hand rest gently at the back of my
neck. "Did you find one?"

"Maybe."

With a less-than-confident smile, the clerk announced, "I guarantee it, ma'am. This will be in full bloom exactly one week from
today."

"What do you think?" I asked Adam.

"What do I know about houseplants, Steph?"

Sometimes I just can't concentrate when Adam is around, so I
accepted the clerk's guarantee. I wanted everything to be perfect
for Amy's visit. And the miniature rose, with its lush leaves and
dozens of tiny buds, was perfect.

Now, only five days later, things weren't perfect at all. They
weren't even acceptable, to borrow a word from my father, the
English teacher. I let my head drop dramatically to my arms on the
top of the desk in my room. After a fervent moan, I thought I
heard the tiniest of thuds and turned my head so I could see the
rose. Three more petals floated down and settled on the desk. My

sister Amy's gift was disintegrating right before my eyes! Theatrics come easily for me. Did I mention that I'm an actress? In the school play last spring, I played Abby Brewster, one of the spinster aunts in *Arsenic and Old Lace.*

Any minute I expected to hear Mom's rusty, red Toyota sputter down our street and lurch into the driveway. She'd gone to Idaho Falls to pick up Amy and Tyler. Ty is my favorite nephew. Actually, he is my only nephew, and Amy is my only sibling. I hadn't seen either one of them since Tyler was born last May, and he would be five months old on the twenty-second.

I know that it's pretty common for sisters to have relationship problems, especially when they're only two years apart. But Amy has always been my best friend. Even when we were young, she never bossed me around. In the park, she'd let me try all the swings and rings and slides without offering pious words of warning. Of course, on the way home, as we'd approach a busy street, she would reach over and hold my hand tightly. She didn't preach about safety the way my friends' sisters did; she just held my hand.

I had wanted to ride up to Idaho with Mom, but there was hardly enough room for Amy, Tyler, and all their stuff. When you travel with a baby, my mother informed me, it's impossible to travel light.

At three, Mom pulled into the carport and honked. I scooped up the scattered petals and added them to others in a sandwich bag in the desk drawer. I almost broke my leg rushing down the stairs to open the door.

We exchanged the usual animated family greetings. If you happened to catch John Boy coming home from college on *The Waltons,* you'll get the picture. Tyler was cranky but bestowed a reluctant smile on his doting Aunt Stephanie anyway. Amy was still beautiful, but she looked tired.

Later in my room—actually *our* room because we shared it for most of our lives—Amy lay back on her old bed and yawned.

"I thought you would redecorate." She scanned the area. "You could move my bed and dresser out to give yourself more room."

"One of these days I will," I said. "It hasn't even been a year since the wedding."

She sighed. "Somehow it seems longer."

"You look tired."

"With Ty downstairs being spoiled by his grandma, this is the first real break I've had since he was born."

"He takes naps, doesn't he?" I asked.

"Sure, but when he finally settles down, there's always something waiting to be done." She grabbed Mr. Boo Boo, my ancient teddy bear, and hugged him. "When I leave him with Maria in the next apartment—we trade baby-sitting—it's to make doughnuts at the shop on the corner, not exactly a vacation."

I didn't know what to say.

Amy smiled. "Don't pay any attention to me, Steph. Wednesday is my day to whine. I love Tyler with all my heart. He's the most wonderful little person in this whole world. I just didn't realize how demanding motherhood could be." She sat up. "But I love it."

I couldn't tell if she was trying to convince me or herself.

"I almost forgot! I got you a present," I said, "a welcome-home gift." I grabbed the miniature rose with both hands and strutted to the bed, dropping pink petals all the way.

"This is great!" As she took the plant, Amy's face was flushed with surprise. "It's beautiful."

I pulled out the sandwich bag. "Here's the rest of it. It wasn't supposed to bloom until day after tomorrow, but it just couldn't seem to help itself. I guess it was as excited about your visit as I was."

Amy looked at me and laughed. "What were you going to do, glue these back on?"

"I was going to take it back to Buds 'n' Blossoms and trade it for a new one," I said, "one with more self-control. But this one's shape is so perfect, and I was afraid—"

"It is perfect!" Amy interrupted. "Thanks, Steph. This is the nicest gift I've ever received."

She was exaggerating, but I loved her for saying that.

"What's his name?" Only Amy would name a houseplant. She set the rose carefully back on the desk in a shaft of October sunlight. "I'll think of something."

It was wonderful to have Amy home. Almost immediately, it felt as though she had never left. The situation was even better because of Tyler. It seemed as though he came to visit for the sole purpose of making us laugh. When my father came home, we took turns recounting every wonderful thing his grandson had done in the last three hours. "Of course he's extraordinary," Dad said. "Look at his heritage!" He took Ty into the living room and began collecting his own list of Tyler's Terrific Tricks while we started supper.

Later in the evening, I didn't want to leave, not even to join Adam for a movie. Of course, my reluctance vanished as soon as I answered the door. I feel about Adam Worthington Jordan III the way Amy feels about Tyler. I know his name sounds ostentatious. He complains when anyone pronounces the entire flamboyant appellation—another of my father's words. "It sounds like the millionaire on Gilligan's Island," Adam moans. But he deserves every wonderful letter—and number—in that name. Since he's the third, it's clear that the AWJs are definitely getting better.

"Let me see that little guy," he said, taking the baby from my mother. He began mesmerizing Ty with his dark, long-lashed eyes and deep voice. I've been known to succumb to such wizardry myself. His charm is infectious. In seconds, Tyler was smiling and talking to Adam like an old friend.

When he finally looked up and said, "We really ought to go, Steph. The show starts at 7:30," I forgot that I hadn't wanted to leave.

We held hands all the way to the mall, even when Adam had to shift. That takes a certain cooperation which seems natural to us after all this time. We've been Adam-and-Steph around school and church for almost two years. After we parked, Adam leaned toward me. I knew he would. I leaned into him, and our lips met. We had passed the uncertain, self-conscious, clumsy stage long ago. He kissed me gently at first, then with a delicious hint of urgency. He had missed me as much as I missed him.

Kissing Adam is like putting on clean socks: familiar and comfortable, satisfyingly appropriate—but more fun, of course. Sounds corny, right? When it comes to Adam Worthington Jordan III, I am corny. He's handsome and smart and funny without overdoing it. We are meant to be Adam-and-Steph forever. There's college and family and all that other future stuff to work out, but we'll unravel all those puzzles together.

"The movie," I reminded him.

He pulled back to his side of the car. "Right."

Did I hear a sigh?

It was my favorite kind of film, a romantic comedy, and its magic lingered as we drove home. On a school night I'm supposed to be in by 10:30. That means in the house, my father reminds me without fail. We parked in front to . . . talk.

Something was changing between us. When we weren't together, I felt incomplete. Throughout every day, Adam was on my mind. *How would he feel about this? He'd have something funny to say right now. If he were here, I know his face would light up and that intoxicating grin would spread across it.*

And when we were together, especially when we were alone, I felt so close to him. I hadn't asked him if he had the same feelings about me, but I know he did. Every kiss, every touch, just seemed to make that connection stronger. It all felt so wonderfully grown-up, so exhilarating, so apropos—the English teacher, again.

The second time my mother flashed the porch light, I knew I'd better go in. Adam walked around the car and opened the door for me. With his arm around my shoulders, we walked to the porch. One last kiss, and I went inside. I stood leaning against the door until I heard him drive away.

Amy was on the phone at the foot of the stairs. "Me, too," she was saying. "It won't be very long, honey. Time is going by so fast." She listened. "I will. Here's a kiss from him to you." She smacked loudly into the phone. "I'll call you tomorrow night." Another pause. "I'll stay up to make sure you'll be home. I don't mind. I love hearing your voice." She looked over at me and I started up the stairs, embarrassed.

As I reached the top, I heard Amy say, "I love you, too. Take care, sweetheart. Bye."

I entered the bedroom quietly so I wouldn't wake Tyler in the playpen we had set up. As I bumped into the closet door, Amy turned on the light.

I looked around. "Where's our little Tyler-boy?"

She fell onto her bed. "With Mom. She wants to give me a chance to get a good night's sleep for a change."

"I think she wants to spoil Ty as much as she can while you guys are here."

"I think you're right."

I got ready for bed. Later, while I was brushing my hair, Amy cleared her throat.

"Adam's a great guy."

"That's true. Thank you for noticing," I said. "I love it when my excellent taste is acknowledged."

She smiled. "You two were out in front for quite a while. I thought Dad was going to walk out there in his pajamas and bring you in."

"We have so much to talk about."

Her eyebrows rose dramatically; I'm not the only actress in the family. "You were just talking behind those steamy windows?"

"Sure." I blushed. "Talking and—you know." The conversation required an immediate detour. "How's Marc?"

"He's fine. He's lonesome and worn out, as usual." She grabbed Mr. Boo Boo in a hug. "I don't know why I miss him so much. It seems like we hardly see each other when I'm home. He's always working or studying or sleeping."

"Sounds like a fascinating life."

"You'll find out, Steph. Someday you'll be married, and a mother, and your—and Adam will be working two jobs and trying to go to school."

I shook my head emphatically. "No way. Adam and I have a charmed life. Everything has always been just about perfect for us, and we're going to make sure it stays that way."

Amy laughed.

"What's so funny?"

"Believe me, I'm not laughing at you, Steph. I'm just remembering myself saying the same kind of thing less than two years ago."

"You're kidding!"

She was smoothing Mr. Boo Boo's nonexistent fur. "Think back, little sister. Not so long ago, Amy Parks and Marcus Walker were the golden couple of West Hills Fifth Ward and Ridgecrest High. Marc was secretary of the priests quorum. I was president of my Laurel class. Together we cochaired the seniors' float committee for homecoming. We taught social dancing for the stake. We were king and queen of the senior prom. The list of perfects in our lives went on and on. We thought that nothing could ever go wrong. Nothing was ever going to dull our sparkle."

Amy looked at the ceiling. "I'm not sure when it started, but in the midst of all the shining approval I began to hear a soft whisper of uneasiness at the very back of my mind. We just weren't keeping things—certain things—within a responsible scope. Magically those qualms disappeared whenever we got together, really together. I found out later, much later, that Marc was having the same nagging reservations, but we never talked about it. We never took the time to explore the source of those feelings."

She stroked my bear's nubby head for a few more moments, then looked at me and laughed. "I must really be overtired! Let's get to bed. You have school tomorrow, and I have a whole day of trying to keep Mom from ruining my firstborn by holding him every second."

Relieved that our chat had ended, I went to brush my teeth.

Thursday night Adam came over for supper. I watched as he played with Tyler, making him laugh out loud. The others were watching, too. I loved the fact that everyone in my family loved Adam, my Adam.

Friday Amy took Tyler to Marc's parents' house to visit. They stayed all day, getting home after I was in bed. I lay facing the wall, trying to keep my breathing deep and regular. I didn't want to talk about golden couples or whispers of uneasiness or responsible scope.

Saturday morning I kept the conversation general. "How was your visit yesterday?"

"It was great," Amy said. "Contrary to the popular stereotype, my in-laws are not outlaws. I really love them."

"I always thought that Marc's father was so weird."

"Have you taken a good look at Dad?"

As we laughed together, the unfamiliar feeling of tension that had grown between us disappeared.

"Adam and I are going up the canyon. We want to hike the Medicine Bow one last time before it closes for the year. Want to come along?"

"It sounds like fun," Amy said, "but I'm going shopping with Mom and Marc's mother. They want to get Tyler a couple of things. I think they're vying for the title of World's Greatest Grandchild Spoiler."

"You're going to need a trailer to get his stuff back to Idaho."

Sunday we went to church. Since the Walkers are in our ward and everyone wanted to share Tyler, we filled an entire bench. It was hard to concentrate as the baby was passed from person to person throughout sacrament meeting. Finally Tyler made it clear that he had a definite preference for Adam. He's a very discerning little boy.

Amy's visit was drawing to a close almost before I realized it. She had to work at the doughnut shop Monday evening, so Mom was taking her back to Idaho Falls around ten in the morning. There was a strange emptiness in the air Sunday evening. I talked Adam into skipping the fireside at the stake center so we could spend this last night with Amy and Ty. We popped corn and made fudge and played Trivial Pursuit. I guess we were trying to fill the evening with as many activities as possible so we wouldn't think about the coming separation.

Adam left at nine. "I need to finish a paper for English," he explained. At the door he said, "Anyway, Steph, you need some time with Amy alone." He leaned down to give me a kiss. "You know, to discuss girls' stuff! I'll see you tomorrow." He winked. "With bags under your eyes because you two will probably talk all night."

His laugh floated back through the cold air as he walked to the car.

"I love you," I called.

"Accepted, and returned with amplification!"

Later, with Tyler asleep in Mom and Dad's room, Amy packed.

"Thanks again, Steph," she said, nodding toward the miniature rose plant. "I'll think of you every time I look at it."

"Even without—" I began, and she finished with a grin—"Even without a single rose."

I had stopped saving the small, pink petals, but I tossed the sandwich bag to her anyway. "I guess you won't need these."

She set the bag of petals on the bed behind her. "It's funny. I hate to go back to Idaho, and at the same time I can't wait to get back. I miss Marc. Of course, I miss him even when I'm in Idaho. He works so hard. He goes to the university early every morning, then works at the campus bookstore. Most days he comes home for a little while and studies, then he's off to work at Pappy's Pizza. My schedule's less hectic, but I still feel like I'm dropping off the baby next door every time I turn around so I can rush down to Don's Donuts. We don't find much time for one another, not like we used to."

Amy mustered a melancholy smile. "Sometimes I have to admit that I'd love to go back to being the golden couple." She picked up a package of new infant undershirts from the bed. "But not now. Now we have Tyler, and there's no going back."

She stuffed the package into one of her bulging boxes. "I had a long conversation with Marc this afternoon. Dad's going to kill me when he gets the telephone bill."

She paused. "Marc Walker is my best friend, you know? I'm glad we talk about things now. We discussed you and Adam."

I shot her a defensive glare, but Amy came over to sit next to me on my bed. "I finally figured out what I want to say."

Lucky me, I thought.

"Now, Marc warned me. If I say anything preachy to you, he will personally hold me down while you stuff my mouth with cinnamon bears. You know how I feel about cinnamon bears."

She took a deep breath and grabbed my hand. "Here goes. Marc and I were good kids, good LDS kids, with testimonies and all the support that comes with being active in the Church. If someone had suggested that we were doing anything evil or wicked, we would have laughed in surprise. Even now I can't think of any aspect of our loving one another as a sin. But even good kids can lose their perspective. It's so easy to move too fast. Their direction isn't wrong. It's their pace that leads to trouble."

Looking around the room, her gaze finally rested on the desk. "It's like the miniature rose!"

It's what? I thought.

Amy hurried on. "Once the buds start to bloom, there's no way of pushing them back into their green, leafy coats. Once two people start expressing their affection in physical ways, it's almost impossible to go back to not demonstrating that love. You only feel like going on to more mature, more complete expression. You love Adam, and he loves you. That's easy to see. Just don't let that love lure you into doing anything that will make your future harder."

Amy picked up the bag of petals from her bed. "Don't settle for petals by rushing things when by waiting you can have the entire beautiful rosebush. Love and all the expressions of it are worth waiting for. I wish I had truly understood that. I wish I had talked to Marc about it."

She didn't actually cry, but there were tears in her eyes as she dropped the bag into my lap. "That's it! That's all I wanted to say." Standing up, she started packing the last few things as though we'd just been talking about cookie recipes. At last our eyes met. "Was that preachy?" she asked with a grin. "I really hate cinnamon bears!"

Monday after school I found a note taped to the front door. "Steph, look by the toaster!" It was a game we used to play, a kind of treasure hunt. In the kitchen I found another note, and so on all through the house. I came at last to my bedroom.

Sitting on the desk was a brand new miniature rose. Its tiny buds were just opening to display the velvety redness tucked enticingly inside. Suddenly I could almost feel Amy's hand holding mine tightly, keeping me safe from traffic and other dangers.

There was a note, of course. "My dearest Steph. Meet your new plant, Maynard. Remember that I love you! Amy." At the bottom was a hastily scrawled postscript. "If you want to, you can share Maynard with Adam!"

I knew I would.

Paul Pitts is an English as a second language specialist in Jordan School District in Salt Lake City and works to provide support for students who are new to the United States. His experiences with these students and his experiences teaching on a Navajo reservation have influenced many of his novels for young readers. Paul's books include a young adult novel, *For a Good Time, Don't Call Claudia,* and three novels for young readers: *Racing the Sun, Shadowman's Way,* and *Crossroads.* He is currently finishing a mystery, tentatively titled *Wolf Chant.*

three

Fathers
Relationships
Testimony
Decisions

"I know who's my Savior," sobbed the man with the tattoo on his neck.
"He paid the price for me, and I didn't come cheap, let me tell you."

CHURCH IN THE CITY

Kirsten T. Cram

ANDIE MCMILLAN DROVE DOWN Josephine Street, looking for landmarks that would jog her memory. She hadn't paid attention to her dad's directions when he called earlier that morning to wake her up for church. Every other weekend, Andie went to church with her dad; it was part of the custody agreement her parents had settled on last year. This week, however, she would not be attending their regular ward. Her dad had just moved to some grungy apartment downtown and now belonged to an inner-city branch. She was supposed to meet him at the City Park Branch somewhere along Josephine Street just before it intersected with Colfax. Andie was sure she could find the huge, brown Victorian house the Ladies' Guild rented to the LDS Church on Sundays. It must be around here somewhere.

The streets were pretty crowded for a Sunday morning, Andie thought. There were a lot of weird-looking people just kind of standing around. She reached across with her right hand to double-check her door—yes, it was locked. Pulling up to a stop sign, Andie frowned. Her mother didn't make her go to church anymore, and there didn't seem to be any point in going through the motions just for her father's sake. *I mean, it's not as if we're pretending to be a family anymore,* she thought, *so why should I keep up this charade for him?* Besides, she could just imagine who might be attending this branch. Probably a bunch of old people and undoubtedly some of these bums from the street. You always had to watch out for people that just wanted a free ride—they only pretended to be interested

73

in church to get a free meal or some money from the bishop. Her dad would say that was unfair, but hey—it was true. *Welcome to the real world, Dad.* Andie's mind was churning. *If you had figured out how to grow a spine, you and Mom might still be together.*

Andie blinked several times. A tall, skinny man was standing on the other side of the street, waving his middle finger at her. She inhaled sharply. He was yelling at her now and walking in her direction. How long had she been staring at him?

"Oh my gosh!" she screamed, flooring the gas pedal and shooting through the intersection. She fumbled with the car radio, turning up the volume so high that it vibrated the dashboard. As she careened down the street, everything was a blur. It was a miracle she didn't run into someone. And then another miracle—there was her dad's big, green Buick parked on the side of the street and flashing in the sun like a boat in the harbor. Andie stepped on the brakes, swerved a little, and spun into the gated parking lot, her tires spitting gravel.

The meetinghouse belonging to the Ladies' Guild was beautiful and massive. Huge wooden beams and pillars of stone supported the entrance. Andie pulled open the door and wobbled into the foyer. Her heart was still pounding, and she couldn't detect any feeling in her legs. She cleared her throat a few times as the color began to seep back into her cheeks.

A toothless woman with bare, scabby legs who could have been forty or sixty was swaying gently in the entrance to the meeting room. She flashed a brilliant smile, minus the teeth, and crowed, "Oh, have we got a visitor today?"

Andie looked away with a tight-lipped smile. "I'm certainly not one of the regulars," she muttered under her breath. She scanned the meeting room, suddenly anxious for a glimpse of her father.

Brother McMillan was standing beside the sacrament table, talking to a pint-sized man buckled into a wheelchair. As Andie got closer, she realized the man wasn't necessarily as old as he'd appeared from a distance; in fact, there was something about him that seemed almost childlike. He was propped into his chair like an oversized doll, yet his gnarled, groping fingers, deep-set eyes, and graying crewcut gave him a wizened appearance. She stood several feet away from her father, watching him visit with the stumpy little man. They were laughing over one of her dad's dumb jokes. *Why did he take so much time talking to people like that?* she wondered angrily. It was weird how he seemed so comfortable around— well, anyone, really.

Brother McMillan looked up and saw Andie waiting for him. He motioned for her to come over, but Andie shook her head vigorously. She did not feel up to meeting the little man in the wheelchair just yet. Turning away, she plunked down on a chair—the hard, collapsible kind that would probably give her permanent back damage. Andie couldn't believe it, but her old ward in Aurora, with its semicomfortable pews, was starting to look pretty good at this point.

"Hi, honey," said her father, leaning over to kiss her on the cheek. "Do you want to come over and say hello to Dirkie?"

"I don't think so, Dad," she said, flashing him a stony scowl. "The meeting is about to start—that is, if they can get their act together around here." It *did* appear that things were not quite on schedule. An old woman with pale purple hair had just settled at the piano and was sailing through a creative interpretation of "Joseph Smith's First Prayer." Andie looked around to see if anyone else was suffering through the prelude, but no one seemed to notice the mistakes. She dropped her shoulders, shaking her head with disbelief. *Hasn't anyone heard of a signature key around here?* she wondered. With her dad sitting next to her, Andie turned to get a good look around the room.

This looks more like a homeless shelter than an LDS sacrament meeting, Andie thought. Or maybe more like a lockup. She stared at a dark-haired man sitting a few rows back and on the other side of the aisle. He was covered in tattoos. There was even some kind of ominous marking on his neck. He wore jeans and a white shirt with the sleeves rolled up and liberally unbuttoned at the neck. He sat staring into his hands. *I hate to break it to you, bud, but no one here feels like seeing your hairy chest.* Andie looked away, her mouth pinched into a tiny smirk.

A young woman was seated a few chairs away from the tattooed man. She too seemed to be staring but not really seeing anything.

She wore big lavender-framed glasses that perched on the tip of her nose, forcing her to tilt her little face upwards.

Dirkie glided by in his wheelchair. His face, frozen with a permanent expression of happiness and surprise, intercepted Andie's line of vision. She blinked and arched her neck, and the withering smile was back on her face. That look didn't work on Dirkie. His smile grew broader, if that was possible. He seemed pleased to have caught her attention. He rolled on.

Another young woman came in and sat down. She had long, beautiful hair that fell forward, almost covering her face. It was impossible for Andie to see what she looked like, but what really caught her attention was the girl's clothes. She was wearing a skirt that was very short. *Way too short for those hips, honey,* Andie thought, laughing to herself and not hearing the branch president call the meeting to order.

Andie sat up to attention throughout the opening exercises. She tilted her head and tapped her fingernails on her chair, waiting for a little old man dragging an oxygen tank to bring her the sacrament. He shuffled towards her at a rate that was making Andie ache to get up and grab the tray for herself. She managed to keep smiling until the old man's trembling hand caused the little paper cups to shudder and spill a few drops onto her lap. Andie leaned over and took the tray away from him. *Couldn't they at least find someone who still had basic motor coordination skills?* she thought.

Today was fast Sunday. Andie had no idea what to expect. In a regular ward, there is always the token weirdo who gets up each month to call the congregation to repentance, share a revelation, or detail some personal problem. The congregation, girded by normalcy, generally reacts to such awkward moments by exchanging sympathetic glances until the bishop finally intercedes. But a weirdo is always the exception to the rule in a regular ward. Here, on the other hand. . . . Andie took another quick look around the room. *I'm probably the only sane person sitting here,* she thought. *What on earth are these people going to say?*

She didn't have long to wait. No sooner had the time been announced for the bearing of testimonies than a tall, lanky man jumped up and strode down the aisle. He turned abruptly to face the gathering, surveying the room with a wild look in his eyes.

"There's been a lot on my mind lately and no one to say it to," he began, scratching his head and staring at the floor.

Here we go, thought Andie, looking sideways at her dad. As usual, Brother McMillan was too involved in what was going on to catch her sarcastic expression.

"You all know me—Mike Keeton—but I don't think I really knew a lot about you until this past month. I sure do appreciate you people for paying your fast offerings. You people have done me a real favor this month. You know, I think I'm doing a pretty good thing, helping immigrants to read and write. I'm not hurting anybody, at least. But then there's the guy who pays me. Somehow he decided that since there wasn't a lot going on last month, it would be OK to cut my pay in half. In half! Can you believe it? I guess having a master's degree doesn't give me the smarts to know what I can live on and what I can't, because my boss seems to think I'll be just fine. You know, I have a mental disorder where I can't always control my temper, but can you blame me sometimes?"

Great, why not start out with the resident psychopath? Andie thought. *No way does this guy have a master's degree.* She turned and nudged her father, her face spiked with disbelief, but Brother McMillan was busy laughing with the rest of the congregation. She looked to the branch president. He was leaning back in his chair, shaking his head, and smiling, not exactly poised for action. *Isn't anybody going to do anything?* she wondered. *Like maybe call 9-1-1 before this guy decides to lose his temper and strangle someone with the microphone cord?* Andie sat back and folded her arms. Well, she definitely wouldn't be coming back here again. Her dad could use that custody agreement for toilet paper, for all she cared.

"Anyway," Mike continued, "I couldn't have made it through this month without the big boxes of food President and Sister Alexander kept leaving on my doorstep. And I know the money for that food came from the fast offering fund. So I thank you good people for your kindness. I can't be a member of the Church right now because of some—issues. I've talked to President Alexander about those things, and I'm trying to do what it takes to get back into the Church. But I still appreciate that I can come here and say my piece and that you people will listen to me, because there's not too many people that want to listen to me anymore. So that's all I have to say, in the name of Jesus Christ, amen."

On the way back to his seat, Mike had to negotiate around Dirkie's wheelchair. Dirkie was gliding towards the pulpit with the same idyllic expression people often have when they're out enjoying nature. His eyes were half-closed, his mouth was curved in a lazy, almost unconscious smile, and his head rested gently against his shoulder. Even with his long, gnarled fingers and his stumpy, strapped-in body, there was a strange, slow grace to his movements that made everyone else seem awkward instead of Dirkie. He wheeled his chair around and looked into the audience with a delighted smile. He spoke with a lisp.

"Well, I just wanna thay that I know that the Book of Mormon ith a very, very good book. And I'm trying to read it every day. And I know I'm very lucky because I got Nadine to take care of me. She'th a very, very nice lady." Nadine, the woman with the scabby legs, could not purse her lips to keep from smiling. Andie watched her curiously.

"And I know, Lord, that you take care of them that do for themthelves. And I juth want you to know, I'm doing the beth that I can." Dirkie paused, his eyes huge behind the thick lenses of his bifocals. He blinked at the audience, looking very pleased. Then, looking up at the ceiling and straining against his seat belt, Dirkie called out, "I'm with you, Jethuth!" He settled back in his chair, his head nodding gently. "I say theth things in the name of Jethuth Chrith, amen."

The audience responded with an amen and settled into a comfortable silence. Andie looked down at her hands. No one got up. There was a rustle behind her, and she looked up expectantly, but still no one spoke. She glanced over at the branch president. He seemed strangely unconcerned. Andie hated this downtime in a testimony meeting. It was like some guilt-ridden waiting game in which everyone is hoping someone else will get up and put an end to the silence. She coughed and stared at her father's shoes—they had to be big enough for the circus. She used to love wearing his shoes around the house when she was little, clunking and tripping, seeing her parents laugh at her. And the times when her dad came home from work and danced with her around the kitchen, her feet balancing on his big, shiny shoes. That had been fun. Andie's throat began to tighten. She squeezed her eyes shut, trying to push back the wave of emotion that came with her memories.

"I got something to say."

Andie craned her neck sharply towards the sound. It was the man with the tattoo on his neck. He was standing right beside his chair, near the back of the room.

"It's been awhile since I was here. Some of you may know me—my name is Nick Martinez. I don't know why it's so hard for me to make it, but this is the place I know I'm supposed to be. I thank God that—no offense to that first dude, 'cause he said he was tryin'—but I'm thankful that I got a job. At least I can hold up my head and come here only cause I want to and not because I'm lookin' for a handout."

Oh, great, Andie scoffed inside, *let's insult the wacko who can't control his temper.* She rolled her eyes, but her sarcastic thought did not bring its usual shot of self-assurance. She looked around at the congregation. Everyone, including Mike, seemed so relaxed, so peaceful. The tightening feeling crept back into Andie's throat. She swallowed as Nick went on.

"I'll be honest with ya. I'm a bit of a Sunday Christian. I got a problem with drinking—not as bad as it used to be, 'cause I'm trying to kick the habit. But I got a six-pack of Bud back home in my fridge, and I'm just kinda keepin' it there for—I don't know what. I just can't bring myself to throw it away. I don't wanna give it to nobody, neither, cause I don't wanna be adding drama to someone else's life." The audience chuckled with Nick. Andie didn't know whether to be shocked or impressed. How could he be so honest about his problems? Nick cleared his throat and went on.

"Like that first guy said, sometimes life makes you feel a little crazy. Well, welcome to the club! It's a crazy world out there. They say even the sane can be insane, man. I've seen a lot of things in my life. I've been through almost everything you can think of—except murder. And if that's what God wants, hey, bring it on, man. I ain't scared." Nick's voice broke, and he buried his face in his hands.

"I say I ain't scared 'cause I know who's my Savior," he sobbed. "I know Jesus Christ will be there waiting for me when I die. He's the one who died for my sins, man. He paid the price for me, and I didn't come cheap, let me tell you. Ain't no one else can help me get back to heaven. And I know I gotta do my part. I know I gotta live the best I can. Maybe that's why I'm afraid to open that Book of Mormon, because I'm afraid of how it's gonna change my life when I read it."

Nick stopped and drew in a deep breath. He wiped his face with his hands and gave a little laugh. "It's funny. I ain't afraid of nothin', but I'm afraid of that Book of Mormon. You know what I'm sayin'? It's like, I know the scriptures can bless my life, but I'm afraid of how much responsibility they'll bring."

Nick paused. He was staring at the floor. "I guess it's pretty dumb to be afraid of a book, especially for the good it'll bring ya. I guess I better think about that. Amen."

Andie squeezed her eyes shut. She could hear the sounds of sniffling throughout the small congregation, but she didn't want to give in to her own emotions. All of a sudden, everything seemed so tiring, so pointless. She felt old, like she'd been living a hundred years. Her mind raced through a corridor of memories: her mother's constant baiting to provoke her father, his complacent reactions that eventually diffused the situation but never dealt with their problems, the steady withdrawal Andie felt as she watched her family tear apart. It was a retreat that had taken on a life of its own. Isolation became a lens that faded everything she saw into a distance beyond her reach or concern.

Andie shook her head. Sometimes she did that just to get a sense of her own existence, just to see if she was still *there*. She looked at her father's shoes again. They were worn out, not as shiny as she'd remembered them. The memory of dancing on his shoes flashed through her mind again. Things had seemed so perfect then. Andie felt a bitter ache as she visualized that little girl whirling around the room with her father, unaware of the disaster waiting to shatter her happy world. How could life be so hard and out of control? She could still feel herself whirling around, only now there was nowhere to put her feet and the music mocked her and echoed in her ears. It was easier to pretend she didn't care than to try to find some way to stop stumbling around. But deep down Andie had an uneasy feeling that she couldn't afford to avoid reality much longer.

She thought about her vow to tell her dad she wouldn't be coming to church anymore. Would that be a step towards taking some control over her life, or would that only make the music play on? There was a good feeling in this place, she could admit that much. What did she want? For a moment, the great anger inside of her seemed to ebb away and she could feel how tired she was of struggling. This was her decision, her choice, one of the few that was still hers to make. What did she want?

After several more testimonies the little old woman with purple hair was back at the piano, hacking through the closing hymn. It took Andie a few minutes to recognize the tune. Even with its glaring flaws, the music was familiar and faintly calming, not as irritating as it had seemed earlier. Andie sighed. It was hard to understand exactly what she wanted anymore. *I want things to be perfect again,* she thought, ignoring the voice in her mind that reminded her how unrealistic she was being. *I don't care. I don't care. I'm sick of everything.* Andie pushed her thoughts into a corner. She could feel a headache coming on. She let the words and music of the hymn filter back into her mind, without really paying attention to what they meant. The sound was familiar. That was good enough for now.

Kirsten T. Cram was born and raised in Vernon, British Columbia. She graduated from BYU with a B. A. in English teaching in April, 1995, and taught high school English for two years in Denver, Colorado. She has published poetry in *Kinesis, Wasatch Review International,* and *Plainsongs.* She also served a mission in Santa Rosa, California, and is interested in learning foreign languages, and enjoys many sports, especially basketball. She and her husband, Roger, recently celebrated his graduation from law school at the University of Denver and the birth of their first child. They now live in Las Vegas, Nevada.

As members of the Church, we give up an awful lot. Is it worth it?
Travis and Mike consider that question for the first time in their lives.

On the Inside Looking In

Jack Weyland

ORDINARILY YOU DON'T EXPECT TO see an angel in the cultural hall on a Saturday afternoon after four hours playing one-on-one basketball, but that's what happened to Mike Rodriquez and Travis Anderson. They were in the middle of their fifteenth game when a girl appeared, cleared her throat, and called out, "Excuse me."

They turned around, and there she was: tall, beautiful, bare-foot, and dressed in white, just like an angel should be.

"Do either of you know when the baptism is?" she asked.

Travis wiped the sweat from his forehead and sauntered over to get a closer look. Mike was right behind him. "When did you think it was?" Travis asked.

"Four o'clock."

Travis looked at the clock. It was already four thirty. "Are the missionaries here yet?"

"No."

"Then it's probably not at four. Baptisms never start more than fifteen minutes late."

"I don't suppose you know when it will be, do you?"

"Not really."

"Well, OK. Thanks anyway." She left the gym.

"Holy cow, did you get a look at her?" Mike asked.

"She's OK, I guess," Travis said.

"Are you crazy? She's a lot more than just OK. Let's go talk to her."

"We're not finished with the game yet," Travis said.

"What difference does it make? We've already played about ten thousand games today."

"Maybe so, but this one is for the championship of the world."

"You said the last one was for the championship of the world. And I won that one."

Travis sighed. He hated to lose. "But *this* game is for the championship of the entire universe."

"I'm tired, and my feet hurt."

"That's no excuse," Travis said.

"I don't care. You're not going to talk me into playing another game. I quit. I'm going to talk to that girl."

Travis followed Mike out of the cultural hall. "Fine, but if you walk out in the middle of the game, that means I won," Travis said. "I am the champion of the entire universe."

"Yeah, whatever," Mike said.

They found her on the sofa in the foyer. She was reading a paperback copy of the Book of Mormon.

"We came to talk to you," Mike said.

"Yeah," Travis added, using his recently acquired deep voice. "In case you wanted to talk to some *real* men."

She looked at Travis. "Have you got a cold?"

"Not really, why?"

"Just wondering." She laid her book on her lap. "Is there any chance the missionaries might have forgotten about the baptism?" she asked.

"Never happens," Mike said. "Baptisms are all they live for."

"They said they'd call if there was a change in time." She gave a frustrated sigh. "They probably called, but I'm staying with my brother, and he's so set against me joining your church he probably didn't tell me they had called."

"If you want, we could make a phone call and find out for sure when it is," Mike said.

"That'd be great." She smiled warmly.

They both left to phone. "She is so awesome!" Mike said in the hallway.

"She's all right. You know what, though? I really think she likes me," Travis said.

Mike laughed. "Yeah, right. I'm sure she's totally crazy about you." He mimicked her asking Travis if he had a cold.

"All I'm saying is she likes me," Travis said.

"So? She likes me too."

"Maybe so, but she likes me better," Travis said.

"No way," Mike said. "But why don't you tell her you're champion of the entire universe? I'm sure she'd be really impressed by that."

They called the ward mission leader and returned to the girl.

"The baptism is scheduled for six," Mike said.

"Six?" She glanced at her watch. "I guess I'll just stay here and wait."

"We'll wait with you," Travis said, sitting down next to her.

"Thank you. By the way, I'm Brittany Stevens."

"I'm Travis. And this is Mike."

"Nice to meet you. You guys are being so nice to me."

"No problem. So, what year in school are you?" Mike asked.

"I'm a sophomore."

"Yes!" Travis grinned. "We're sophomores too."

Brittany looked confused. "In college?"

"College?" Travis's voice cracked. "Well no, not exactly college."

"So you're sophomores in high school, right?"

"Well yeah, but we're very mature for our age," Mike said. "Ask anyone. They'll tell you."

"That's right," Travis added. "Except I'm just a little more mature than Mike here."

"No way," Mike said.

"You guys are cute," Brittany said.

"Cute?" Travis frowned. "That's probably the worst thing you could say."

"Why?" Brittany asked.

"Kittens are cute. Bunnies are cute," Mike said. "We don't want to be cute."

"What do you want to be?"

"Macho men," Travis said in his deepest voice. It sounded more like a growl.

Brittany smiled. "You'll grow out of it. Let me ask you guys a question. Have you been members of the Church all your lives?"

"Yeah, we have."

"What advice can you give me about being a member of the Church?"

Travis answered first. "Well, if you're in a class and one of the bishopric comes in and says they want some people to be on the program for sacrament meeting, raise your hand right away and tell him you'll say the prayer. That way you won't be asked to give a talk."

"OK," she said, a little confused. "What else?"

"You need to know some things about potluck suppers," Mike said, "because we have a lot of those in our church. The first rule is don't fill up on noodles. Go for the meat and desserts."

Brittany tried not to smile. "I'll make sure I remember that."

"One more thing about potlucks," Travis added. "Sometimes people who come late to a potluck feel guilty because they didn't have time to cook anything, so a lot of times they'll stop and pick up something really good. Like our last potluck, somebody came late and brought a whole bucket of extra-crispy chicken. But by that time most people were already full. Not Mike and me. No sir. We took full advantage of the situation. Man, between the two of us we ate pretty much the entire bucket. It was great."

"What we're saying," Mike said, "is that at a potluck it's real important to pace yourself. You never know what food is coming late, and you've got to be prepared."

"Thanks, guys. These are things the missionaries didn't bring up. I'm sure they'll be very helpful. Anything else?"

"Yeah, sure," Travis said. "When you're in Sunday School class, remember that it's important for the class not to answer every question the teacher asks."

"Why?"

"I can see we need to walk you through this. A lot of converts mess up on this one. Let's say I'm the teacher, OK? So I ask a question like, What book in the Old Testament is quoted a lot in the Book of Mormon?"

"Isaiah, right?" she answered.

"Right, but even if you know the answer, don't say anything. Just stare at the floor like you're trying real hard but you can't even begin to understand the question. And everybody's got to do that, OK? So what happens? The teacher figures the question is too hard. So she asks an easier question."

Brittany nodded tentatively.

Travis continued. "So anyway, because nobody answered the first question, the teacher asks something easier. And nobody answers that either. The thing is, if you keep this going, the questions get easier and easier. Usually after about five questions, you can get it down to something like, Who can tell me what day of the week we go to Sunday School?"

Brittany laughed. "Anything else?"

"It's always good to know a little kid you can take out of sacrament meeting," Mike said.

"Especially on the second Sunday of the month," Travis said.

"Why the second Sunday?"

"That's when the speaker from the high council comes," Mike said.

"What does he talk about?" Brittany asked.

Mike shrugged his shoulders. "I don't know. I'm always out in the hall with my little sister by the time he really gets going. I pity the people without little kids to take out."

"I don't have any younger brothers or sisters, so I have to stay in the meeting," Travis said. "Usually the high council speaker has about eight books and he drops the entire stack on the podium and the sound rumbles through the chapel, so everybody knows it's going to be a really long talk. And then he tells us what the topic for the month is, and then he reads what the dictionary says about it. So I'm thinking, if this guy had to look up the word in the dictionary to know what it meant, what are the chances he's going to tell us anything we don't already know? By that time I put my head on the pew in front of me and close my eyes and try to get some sleep."

Brittany didn't smile. And that worried Travis. Maybe they'd gone too far. "Is anything wrong?"

"I'm just wondering if I'm doing the right thing. See, the thing is my family is really against me joining the Church. And my friends at college. And the guy I was seeing walked out when he saw all the changes I was making in my life. Right now I don't have any friends except the sister missionaries, and one of them is being transferred next week. So sometimes I ask myself why I'm doing this. You guys have been in the Church all your life, right?"

They nodded.

"Is this church worth losing all your friends and your family over?"

Travis couldn't answer. Things had always been easy for him. His parents had been encouraging him all his life to be true and faithful to the things the Church taught. He wasn't sure if he even had a testimony.

"It *is* worth it," Mike said. "The things the missionaries told you are true."

"Are you sure of that?" she asked.

Mike cleared his throat. "I'm sure."

"What about you, Travis?"

Travis felt like there was a circle and he'd always been outside it. Now was the time to take a stand.

He sighed and said softly, "I'm sure."

She smiled at them. "Thanks, you guys. That's just what I needed."

Two missionary cars pulled into the parking lot. Two sister missionaries and two elders got out of their cars and started up the sidewalk.

"Is there any chance you guys could come to my baptism?" Brittany asked.

"You bet," Mike said. "We'll run home and change—we live just across the street—and be back in ten minutes."

"That'd be great, but there's one more thing. I'd really like it if you both could be on the program too."

"I'll give the opening prayer," Travis said quickly. He turned to Mike and grinned.

"That would be wonderful. Mike, could I ask you a special favor?"

"You want me to give the closing prayer?"

"No. I was wondering if you could baptize me."

"You want me to baptize you?" His voice cracked.

"Can you do that?" she asked.

"Well, yeah, I'm a priest so I guess I could, but—"

"The sisters taught me about the Church, but I don't even know the elders. You two are my only other friends in the Church right now. Please?"

Travis and Mike moved a short distance away so they could talk. "I don't know how to baptize somebody," Mike whispered.

"Call the bishop to see if it's OK. He and the elders can teach you how to do it."

"What if I mess up?"

"You won't mess up. C'mon, you've got to do it. We're her only friends in the Church."

Mike paused and then returned to Brittany. "I guess I'll go ahead and do it."

"Thanks. That'll really mean a lot to me."

Forty-five minutes later the baptismal service began. They sang a song, and then Travis got up to say the prayer. He looked around. Bishop Romney was there. So were the elders and the sister missionaries. Mike and Brittany sat in front, dressed in white. Travis's mom and dad sat in the back.

They were going to invite Brittany over for ice cream and cake after the baptism. Travis had insisted on refreshments. He'd had ice cream and cake after he was baptized.

He figured Brittany deserved it too.

Jack Weyland is the author of *Charly,* the all-time best-selling novel for LDS teenagers. He has published fourteen other novels and four books of short stories for LDS youth. In addition, over fifty of his short stories have been published in the *New Era.* Jack earned a Ph.D. in physics from BYU and for many years taught physics at the South Dakota School of Mines and Technology. He now teaches physics at Ricks College, and he and his wife, Sherry, live in Rexburg, Idaho.

When you've been LDS all your life, it's easy to take your religion for granted.
What do you do when your best friend, a Catholic,
starts to gain a testimony of his own?

SINK OR SWIM

Adrian Robert Gostick

LANNY MCDONALD O'BRIEN and I were born Newfies.

In 1978, just before I was born, my family moved to Wolf Point and bought the old house overlooking the harbor, next door to the O'Briens. Lanny and I arrived in the world a month apart. Living so close, I guess we *had* to be friends.

Where we grew up is a remote part of Newfoundland near the channel port of Basques and fifty-five minutes by boat from the nearest LDS church. On the Rock it's cold and wet all the time. So cold that at night, before your body has a chance to warm them, the sheets on your bed are slick as ice. So cold that we leave our front doors unlocked because keys can break off in the frozen locks. So cold—well, you get the idea.

For a long time my family and I were the only Mormons in this fishing outport. Then the missionaries arrived on our end of the island, and the Hagens and Alberts joined. So then every week we'd all get dressed in our Sunday best and make the boat ride to church. It was very strange to see the women in their dresses, the men in their suits, and the missionaries standing on the bow all splashing through the dark-green ocean toward Basques.

I've been LDS all my life. But I remember wondering why the Hagens and the Alberts joined, why anyone would join the Church just to spend every Sunday boating to church and back. Sure, there were some cute girls at meetings, but the Hagens and Alberts were old and married. I didn't get it.

But I'm getting ahead of the story.

The spring Lanny was born, the Toronto Maple Leafs were in the quarterfinals of the Stanley Cup play-offs, led by the play-making defense of Borje Salming, the quick goaltending of Mike Palmateer, and the scoring touch of right-winger Lanny McDonald.

Mr. O'Brien was a big Maple Leafs fan. In fact, while his wife was delivering in the hospital in Basques, Mr. O'Brien watched game seven of the quarterfinals in the waiting room. By the time the doctor came out to say "It's a boy," the Maple Leafs and the New York Islanders were locked in a 1–1 overtime battle.

The doctor, who liked a good game of hockey as much as the next Newfie, stayed. And finally when the CBC announcer screamed in a breathless frenzy that Lanny McDonald had scored to advance the Leafs to the semifinals against the Montreal Cana- dians, both the doctor and Mr. O'Brien had the same idea: The kid's name must be Lanny McDonald O'Brien.

They both signed the birth certificate before Mrs. O'Brien had a chance to slap them.

Lanny and I never talked about religion. He was a Catholic, but his family went to church only at Christmas and Easter. He knew I was a Mormon, but for the last few years I'd been less and less excited about it. And Lanny knew better than to bring it up.

But one Saturday during the winter when we were sixteen, al- most seventeen, something changed all that.

I was walking back from the store. My little brother, Tom, was behind me. He was tired and was kicking snowballs the plow had left along the middle of the road.

"Move it," I told him.

"I um," Tom whined deeply, his nose full. He looked up at me and gave me a pathetic smile. I rolled my eyes but bent down, and he ran and jumped onto my back. When we turned down our road, I began to jog. Behind me my brother laughed and covered my eyes with his wet gloves.

"Hey!"

We spun and landed in a yaffle—that's Newfie for a jumble— in the slushy snow in front of Lanny's house.

"Huh, huh . . . huh, huh, huh," Tom laughed.

That's when I noticed them—a couple of bikes leaning up against the side of the O'Briens' house. It was strange. Who would ride bikes in one of our rare snowstorms? Then I noticed two figures in the O'Briens' window. Two guys in dark suits. Familiar faces.

Then it hit me. The missionaries were in Lanny's living room, standing in front of the fire to warm themselves like they belonged.

"Cum onnnn," said Tom. He was standing a couple of meters away flapping his arms up and down.

"Yeah, yeah."

I pulled my gaze away from the window, and we trudged the last few meters home.

On Saturday nights Lanny usually stopped at my house and we'd wander down to the town building, where they'd play a movie or have a dance. That night he knocked about seven o'clock, and I grabbed my coat. We dug our hands in our pockets and walked outside. Since it was too early to be seen at the dance, we headed down toward the harbor.

The wind had been blowing in snow from the island all day, and it was dumped in little drifts in front of every one of the blue and yellow houses. As we crunched along, the wind began to die and the beginnings of a fog started moving in from the ocean.

Lanny began whistling between his teeth. He couldn't whistle very well, and he did it only when he was nervous.

"You ever get sick? I mean really sick?" he asked me.

That's how Lanny McDonald O'Brien started out most conversations, with a question about something he'd been thinking up all day. He was always thinking, always wondering about something.

"You ever see me go to the hospital?" I asked him back.

"I guess not."

"Then you know the answer."

We walked a little more before he said, "I was just thinking I could be a doctor one day."

"I guess. I could see you cutting people up, taking out stuff, charging them lots of money."

He laughed. "Yeah, I could do that."

We walked a bit more, thinking about Dr. Lanny McDonald O'Brien, until he said, "Those Mormon guys came over today."

Lanny took a glance at me to size up my mood, then added, "Said your parents sent them."

That ticked me off, and he noticed my face redden. "My parents sent 'em?"

"That's what they said."

"I'm gonna—gosh, I'm sorry."

He shrugged. "I don't care. It didn't bug me."

We rounded the fence at the bottom of Main and jumped the ballycater—Newfie for the icy fringe—at the edge of the dock. The snow hadn't settled on the rough boards, and we took two to a step. Farther along we walked into the cold ocean fog that hung like a veil. We were alone. No one came out on the dock on a winter night.

"They want to come back again," said Lanny.

"Who?"

"The missionary guys."

"They always do," I said. "That's their job, to come back and back until you join."

"Join what?"

"The Church. The Mormon church."

"Nah, they didn't say that," said Lanny. "They were just visiting."

I laughed. "One of those guys is from the States. You think he came to Wolf Point to talk Maple Leafs hockey with your dad?"

Lanny shrugged.

"What part of the States?" he asked.

"I don't know. They give you a lesson?"

"I guess. They talked a lot."

"They teach you how to pray?"

"Yeah."

"That's the first discussion. They want you to join," I said.

"Hmmmm."

We reached the end of the pier and leaned on the rail, the same rail that one winter Lanny had licked to see if his tongue would really stick to frozen metal. It did. And for a month Lanny had talked with a lisp.

We stared out at the icy water, but it was too dark and the fog was too thick to see much.

"OK, I got a question," said Lanny, nodding his head.

"Always."

"The Mormon guys said the Book of Mormon is like the Bible. I know that's not right 'cause it says at the end of the Bible that there isn't supposed to be anything added to the Bible."

We had talked about that in Sunday School once, but I couldn't remember the answer. "Well, um—"

"And they told us about the guy who said he saw God and started the Mormons."

"Joseph Smith."

"Yeah, I thought it was Brigham Young. Anyway, how does anybody know he didn't just write the book himself?"

"Well, there were a bunch of witnesses who saw the plates he wrote it from," I said.

"Yeah, they were probably Mormons too. Do you guys pray to him?"

Lanny kept asking questions, most of which I couldn't answer. My first instinct was to defend the Church. But he was my friend. I should tell him how I really felt, that I wasn't even sure if I believed anymore, that I was kind of embarrassed to be a Mormon.

I drew in a breath, ready to tell him everything—but I couldn't. From somewhere inside I felt the need to do something I hadn't done in a long time: say a prayer.

I opened my mouth to say something, but I didn't have the words.

OK, I thought, *I'll pray.*

So as Lanny talked I silently told Heavenly Father that I didn't know if the Church was true or not, and I didn't really know what to say.

I waited a few seconds. No answer. I opened my eyes. Lanny had stopped talking and was looking out to the harbor. He was squinting, trying to focus on the dim lights of a trawler that was bobbing in and out of view in the fog.

I don't know why, but I guess that was the moment when everything started making sense.

Lanny needed the gospel, just like I did. We were young. Our lives were confusing. The gospel would answer questions we both had about where to go, who to become.

This time, as I opened my mouth I felt a peace that I hadn't felt since I was a kid. "At church once, some old guy told a story," I began. "It's about a kid who's eighteen and goes to work on a fishing boat out of St. John's. And sometime in the summer of his first year on the boat it hits a sandbar and sinks. Most of the crew climbs aboard the lifeboat, but this guy and the captain get caught by a current and pulled away. They don't have life jackets or anything, and for a long time they just tread water, hoping for someone to find them."

"Wow," said Lanny, who had been on enough fishing boats to know how big the ocean was and how impossible it would be to find anyone swimming in it.

"Anyway, finally the captain realizes that the water's too cold for them to last much longer, so he swims over to the kid and says, 'We're not gonna make it.' And he asks the kid if he's religious. Well, the kid is just like me. He's a Mormon, but he's been kind of goofing off and it's been a while since he's been active. But he says he'll say a prayer for 'em."

"And what happened?"

"He and the captain close their eyes, and the kid says a prayer out loud. And when they open their eyes they see the light of a buoy. They swim over and hang on, and a few hours later they're found."

Lanny smiled. "And the guy telling the story turns out to be the eighteen-year-old kid, right?"

"Uh, no. The guy telling the story was the captain. He joined the Church."

"Hmmm."

I pulled my hands out of my pockets and stuffed them back in again, not sure what to say next. I was feeling guilty for my years of goofing off, for not being able to answer Lanny's questions. But somehow I knew it wasn't too late.

"You said the missionaries told you how to pray. Did they say a prayer too?" I asked.

"Yeah, but no one was drowning."

"Wise guy. How did it make you feel?"

"I don't know. I didn't think about it." He looked out to the ocean and breathed out. "OK, maybe I thought about it."

I turned to him, my eyes wide. "And?"

"Before I left tonight I prayed by myself."

That night, instead of climbing in bed I opened my desk drawer and pulled out my copy of the Book of Mormon. I flipped through the pages. They were filled with red and yellow high-lighter, but I realized it had been a long time since I'd studied what was in there.

It was a story. It was a light in the darkness.

I began to read.

Adrian Robert Gostick began his writing career as the editor of a small-town newspaper in British Columbia, Canada. He has since worked as a writer/editor for the *New Era* magazine, and now works in corporate communications in Salt Lake City. He is the author of the young-adult novels *Eddy and the Habs* and *Impressing Jeanette*. He has won five Utah Golden Spike Awards for writing. Adrian was born in England and raised in Canada. He has a B. A. in journalism from Brigham Young University.

four

Fathers
Relationships
Testimony
Decisions

Jonathan Nelson, a talented young basketball player,
makes a hasty decision,
one he may regret the rest of his life.

BASKETBALL BLUES

A. P. Bowen

I SLAM INTO THE HEAVY DOOR WITH my shoulder, using more force than necessary to push it open, to escape the school building. It feels good to hit something. The icy air outside stings my nostrils and cuts into my lungs, feeling like millions of tiny glass shards as I take a deep breath. I shift the weight of my backpack, then I take my gym bag, wondering why I ever bothered to buy a new one, and I hurl it across the dead grass as far as I can. It lands with a thud thirty feet away.

For an instant, I think about leaving it there and going home without it, then I recognize that the basketball shoes inside cost me hours and hours of pay. And I'll need them for church ball.

I glance around to see if anyone noticed my act of frustration. Three girls I don't know are talking over by the other entrance. Two guys, one of whom I recognize from another ward in town, are climbing into the back seat of a red car driven by somebody's mom. The last school bus is pulling out onto the street. No one seems to have noticed me. Thank goodness.

I shuffle across the lawn and pick up my bag, feeling a little foolish. It's actually rather uncharacteristic of me to throw things around—in public, at least. Still, it felt good to heave it, to do something physical in response to the anger and disappointment I feel.

Picking up my bag, I make a beeline for our beat-up Chevy truck sitting in the middle of the parking lot. I'm grateful Dad let

me drive in to school today. I wonder if he suspected I'd be cut
from the team this afternoon, or if letting me take the truck this
morning was his way of showing a vote of confidence that I'd need
it to get home after varsity practice.

The truth is, I figured I'd be driving home in the dark tonight
after a nice sweaty workout in the gym with the other guys. I was
certain I'd find my name on that white piece of paper hanging on
the locker-room door after school. I'd carefully delayed my arrival
at the gym after my last class so I could read the final team roster
with some privacy yet not be late for practice.

I feel my face flush again as it did when I read the list. Twice.
Twelve names posted, in alphabetical order. I expected to see
mine halfway down: Nelson, Jonathan. Instead, the list went from
Kellerman to Potter. No Nelson.

I unlock the truck and throw my bags on the seat. How could I
have deluded myself into thinking I'd actually made this team? I
climb behind the cold steering wheel and slam the door soundly.
Then I hit the steering wheel so hard it hurts my hand. I swear,
breaking a promise I made to myself months ago to stop profan-
ing. I swear again. I don't care. I'm failing at every other goal I've
set for my senior year—why not this one?

I fish the truck keys out of my jeans pocket, but I don't stick
them in the ignition. I don't want to head home. Not yet. I don't
want to drive up the lane in full daylight and have to face Mom in
the kitchen and explain why I'm home early. I don't want to be
home before Dad gets in from the bank. I don't want to hear Mom
intercept him on the back porch and explain why the truck is already parked outside the barn.

I don't want to face my younger sisters at the dinner table and
explain to them that they're not going to be watching this brother
play basketball at the city high school. Why there won't be any
evening family outings into town to watch me play basketball, like
we all used to do for David's games.

David. For the first time since he left three months ago, I'm actually glad he's out on his mission. I'm relieved that I don't have to
see him, to tell him that I've failed once again to live up to the glorious reputation he established while he was attending high school

here. This way I won't have to hear him say something patronizing, trying to be helpful.

I know Mom will write to him and tell him I didn't make the team. And I know David will try to write something comforting or inspiring back to me, but I'll just avoid reading his letters for a few weeks to spare myself the humiliation. For the millionth time, I feel inadequate: Jonathan Nelson, wimpy younger brother of the great David.

I stare at the brick wall of the gym. What a waste. What a stupid waste of time. Of effort. Of planning. Of transferring from the county high school into this city school for my senior year with the hope I could play basketball on this team with this coach. Of working out in back of the house, shooting free throws, practicing my jump shot and my layups. Of running wind sprints up and down the long driveway from the highway up to our house. All for what? For this fine opportunity to be sitting outside the high school gym on a brilliantly clear winter afternoon facing the fact that I'm not going to play varsity basketball. Ever. I'm not going to wear a gold and green uniform. I'm not going to be part of a team of talented players. I'm not going to get the second chance I've waited for and worked for ever since—

I don't want to complete that thought. I shelve it. I stick the key in the ignition and press the gas pedal, hearing the familiar choke then roar of the truck's noisy engine. The radio blasts music into the cab. I reach for the knob and turn up the volume until I can feel the bass vibrating through the frame of the truck. I hope the music will fill my mind and drive out all the unpleasant thoughts and memories that are lurking there.

Time to move. To get out of here. I back out of the parking space, then I weave through the remaining cars in the lot like I'm playing dodge-cars. At the stop sign I brake momentarily, then I pull out onto the street and gun the engine till I'm roaring down the street. I don't care if I'm speeding.

I pass the school and the drugstore and then the bank. I hope Dad is busy in his office and doesn't see me fly by. But it doesn't really matter. Someone in this town will see me and tell him, "I saw that younger son of yours in the truck yesterday speeding right through the middle of town." There's no such thing as privacy if you're in town. Everybody thinks everything that goes on is their business. Drives me nuts.

I think of the night when the Reids and I filled Lisa's car with grass clippings. The next day everyone in town knew we'd done it. The memory of the three of us guys out in her garage quietly dumping lawn bag after lawn bag of grass clippings through her sunroof makes me smile. Now, that was fun.

Then I think of Matt Reid, and I stop smiling. Matt made the team. I know he'll feel awful about my being cut. He'll call me tonight when he gets home from practice. I know he will. I don't want to talk to him. I don't want to hear him say he's sorry I didn't make it. How he feels responsible for talking me into transferring schools. For trying again.

Trying again. There it is. The memory of my basketball nightmare at the county high school springs to life. I try to shove it back, to get it behind a door in my mind where I can lock it up, but it escapes. I keep seeing myself and the other guys in the blue and white uniforms running Coach Schmidt's plays.

The light ahead turns red. I don't want to stop and wait for it to change, so I hit the blinker and make a rolling stop, then I turn right. I want to keep moving. I don't care if this route home takes twice as long. Suits me just fine.

As I head through a tidy residential neighborhood toward outlying farms, I see the guys in blue and white uniforms again, playing on a hardwood court in my memory. Too late to lock them up. I can tell I'm not going to be able to avoid the haunting replay. Not today.

But I can control my thoughts, I tell myself. I'll allow myself to think about playing for the other high school, but I'll concentrate on the good stuff.

The fact is I'd had fun trying out as a sophomore. Even though I hadn't hit my growth spurt yet and was one of the shortest guys in my class, I'd been a scrappy player, good enough to make the team. At first I loved being on that team. I loved staying after school to practice. I loved hearing the sound of balls bouncing as we ran our drills and the squeak of gym shoes against the hardwood floor when we scrimmaged. I loved the feeling of pounding down the floor, dribbling around other players toward the key. I loved standing at the free-throw line and hearing the swish of the net when the ball dropped through after I'd sent it arcing perfectly through the humid gym air.

I loved joking around with the guys after practice as we showered and dressed in the locker room that smelled of perspiration and damp cinder blocks. I loved walking out into the dark to meet my dad when he came to pick me up from practice. I loved chatting with him each evening as we drove the eight miles back to the farm.

But I didn't love sitting on the bench during that first game. No, I did not. And I did not love Coach Schmidt. Even if he had been friends with Dean Smith and even though he had a great reputation for building winning teams out of slim pickings year after year after year, I did not respect him.

I thought Coach Schmidt was an idiot. I thought he was blind. I thought he was overlooking my brilliant ballhandling and quick, Muggsy Bogues-like moves. I thought he should have his head examined for not giving me the chance to start that game.

Frustrated, I sat there on the bench listening to Coach Schmidt yell at the players on the court. I knew I could outplay any of them. When someone missed a shot or rebound, I did an instant replay in my mind imagining how I would have performed better. And each time the refs blew the whistle, I waited eagerly to hear Coach Schmidt call my name to put me in the game.

But he didn't call my name. At the end of the first half, we were ahead by four points and I was so frustrated from sitting on the bench doing nothing that I wanted to run around the gym to release some energy rather than duck into the locker room for a halftime chat.

During halftime, Coach Schmidt didn't even look at me. Instead he talked to the five players who had played the entire first half as if they were the only five guys alive on the planet. Before we headed back into the gym, I stalled for a second to get a drink while debating whether to say something to the coach, to ask him to put me in the game. I decided it would be better to remain silent.

When we reentered the gym I remember seeing my dad sitting halfway up on the bleachers. So he'd come to watch my first game, just as he'd attended all of David's games in town. I loved Dad for being there. Then I tried to send telepathic messages to Coach Schmidt willing him to let me play so that my Dad would be rewarded for coming.

In the middle of the fourth quarter, Rick Mazuri drew a charging call, putting the other team at the free throw line, and Coach Schmidt was furious. He called a time-out and glanced down the bench. I met his eyes and prayed that he'd call my name.

"Nelson, get in there," he yelled. "Mazuri, sit down!"

My heart raced as I ran onto the court and positioned myself behind the shooter at the top of the key. The guy made both shots, and I heard Coach Schmidt curse from the sideline.

From under the basket, our center threw the ball in to me. I knew which play to run, a pick-and-roll. I dribbled down the court, scrambling around the guy defending me. I was supposed to throw the ball to the forward who posted up and then go set a screen. But when I reached the top of the key, I saw that Todd Murphy, the other guard, had broken free of his man and was wide-open in the lane, so I threw the ball to him. Todd was not expecting the pass, so he turned just as the ball reached him and I was horrified to watch the ball hit his shoulder and bounce into the hands of the other team's forward, who dribbled straight down the sideline, passing within inches of Coach Schmidt's feet, and drove to the basket for an uncontested layup.

The score was tied, and Coach Schmidt immediately called another time-out. I heard him yell my name, and I ran toward him. He pointed to the bench and told Craig Adams to replace me. I felt sick. I dropped onto the bench, and Coach Schmidt marched down to face me. "You are supposed to run the play, Nelson!" he bellowed. "I call the plays, and you run them! That's what you do when you're in the game, do you understand? Now, I don't ever want to see you in there again thinking that you know more than I do. Do you hear me?"

I wanted to die on the spot. I wanted him to shut up and stop yelling. I was certain every person in the gym could hear him. I also wanted to argue back, "Todd was open!" But I didn't say anything. What was the point? I'd finally gotten in the game, and I'd made a mistake within seconds. *Yet,* I told myself, *Todd was wide-open and could have made a great play if he'd only seen the ball coming at him.*

I spent the rest of the game staring at my feet or at the clock. The seconds dragged by. I couldn't believe that Coach Schmidt would pull me after one play. One mistake. He was such a jerk. When the final buzzer sounded, we were ahead by five points. Good. At least he couldn't blame me for losing the game.

In the locker room, Todd said, "Hey, Jon. Sorry I missed that pass. Didn't see it coming." I heard someone else say, "Yeah, Nelson, great pass!" and laugh, but I didn't turn to see who it was.

Dad was waiting for me in the gym. "Your team looked good!" he said as we walked outside. "That was a close game, and you guys pulled it out." He didn't say anything about my solitary play or my wayward pass. I was grateful for his diplomacy.

I don't know when it was that I decided to quit the team. I've tried to replay that next day in my mind, but I can't pull up the exact moment when I made my decision. All I remember is I decided not to go to practice that next afternoon. Instead, I caught the school bus home.

Mom was surprised to see me. "No practice?" she asked as I passed through the kitchen and headed downstairs to my room. I didn't answer, and she didn't ask again. In fact, no one in my family brought up the subject. I simply stopped going to basketball practice, and the topic was never mentioned in our home again.

At school I felt uncomfortable anytime I saw someone on the team. A couple of times I was asked what happened, but I just shrugged in response. Whenever I passed Coach Schmidt in the hall, I looked the other way. The truth is I was embarrassed by my actions. But I was also angry at Coach Schmidt for being such an idiot.

David did say something to me months later. It was in the spring, and we were shooting hoops out in the driveway for the first time after all the snow melted. We were playing horse, and I was actually winning. David asked rather casually as he took a shot, "So whatever happened with Coach Schmidt? Did he drop you from the team?"

"Nope," I responded as I went to retrieve the ball, "I quit."

David didn't reply for a moment. He let me take my shot, then when he had the ball again he dribbled for a long time like he was considering a tricky move. He glanced at me, then he said, "Too bad you didn't stick with it and let Coach Schmidt teach you. He knows the game." Then he drove past me and dunked the ball in the basket, hanging on the rim for a few seconds.

I ignored what he said. David didn't understand. He didn't know Coach Schmidt. He'd chosen to drive into the city so he could attend school with everyone in his seminary class—and play for the big glory team, of course.

And that's what I had decided to do in September, as well: to go to school with most of the other Church kids. And, since I'd grown ten inches in two years and had practiced like crazy on the church team and in my driveway, to try to play basketball with the best team in the county.

So much for that dream.

I look at my watch, surprised to see how early it is still. I'm driving past winter-barren farm fields, and I wonder what I'm going to do with all these empty afternoons now that I won't be staying after school to play ball. There won't be much work to do on the farm until it's time to plant.

I decide I might as well drive by the lake and see if there are any ducks stupid enough to be here in the area when it's this cold and this late in the year.

I quickly glance behind the seat to see if there's a shotgun there. No such luck. Dad probably cleaned all the guns and locked them in the gun cupboard when the season ended last week.

When I reach the turnoff to the lake, I'm relieved to see there are no other vehicles parked along the road. I roll down my window, letting the radio blast into the crisp air, and I honk my horn with a quick staccato beat, trying to scare something into the sky. Only a couple of crows fly in response. No ducks today.

I pull off the road onto the frozen mud of the parking area and kill the engine. I climb out of the truck, slamming the door behind me, then I head through the brush to the shores of the lake.

The water is silver in this afternoon light. The wind that stings my face has swept the surface of the lake, creating a texture that looks like a herringbone pattern. Now I wish I had my camera with me to capture the light and the lake. The wind shifts, and so does the texture of the water. There's a sweep of little ripples and a broad curve of smoother water that looks like etched glass.

I inhale the icy air and hold it in my chest. When I exhale, my breath hangs in front of me like steam. I pick up a couple of rocks and skip them across the water's surface. Three skips. Then five. I watch the tiny concentric circles broaden and expand.

I love this place. It has always felt holy to me. I close my eyes, and for what feels like the thousandth time I thank God for creating such a spot and for letting me live near it. Then I ask God to help me with my pain and this disappointment.

I stop to throw a few more rocks in the lake, then I decide I'd better get on home. As I walk back through the brush toward the truck, I hear David's voice again from the driveway as we played horse. "Too bad you didn't stick with it and let Coach Schmidt teach you."

For the first time in two years, I allow myself to roll that thought around inside my head. I hear David say it again. With David three thousand miles away, I'm glad I don't have to tell him that he was right.

Before I climb into the truck, I stop to look at the lake again. And I wonder where I'd be this afternoon if I had allowed Coach Schmidt to teach me what he knows about the game.

A. P. Bowen, Annette Paxman Bowen, lives in the Seattle area with her husband J. Scott Bowen and their three sons. The author of many articles, Annette's work has appeared in magazines around the world, including the *New Era,* the *Ensign,* and the *Reader's Digest.* Annette is the author of two young-adult novels, *Get A Life, Jennifer Parker!* and *Live and Learn, Jennifer Parker,* as well as a nonfiction book, *Donuts, Letters, and Midnight Phone Calls.* Recently her work has been published in three anthologies, including the best-selling *Chicken Soup* series. She is currently working on a third young-adult novel.

*Two very different young men with very different lives
will discover that they have at least one thing in common.*

FRIENDS IN THE NEWS

Chris Crowe

ミチナガ

IN THE BOTTOM OF MICHINAGA Matsumoto's desk drawer lay a worn copy of the May 1979 *Friend*. Sometimes when he took a break from studying for the upcoming university entrance exams, he dug out the English magazine, a surprise gift from the missionary who baptized him, and thumbed it open to page thirty-eight. He'd done it often enough over the years that the magazine automatically fell open to that page.

His was among the many smiling faces featured in "Friends in the News." Michinaga looked at his picture and read the sentence below it. *Michinaga Matsumoto, 8, Himeji, Japan, recently joined the Church with his mother. He wants to go to college someday.*

He smiled when he recalled the friendly American missionary who ten years ago had surprised him and his friends while they were playing at Himeji Castle. They danced behind the great big *gaijin* and his Japanese companion laughed and shouted "Haro, haro," their version of *hello,* the only English word they knew. It was the first time any of them had seen a real live foreigner, and when he turned around and spoke to them in Japanese, they were so startled that they nearly fell down.

マイク

"Mike. Mike? Are you in your room?"

"Yeah, Mom, I'm studying. What's up?"

"I was cleaning out the bookshelf today, and I found that copy of the Friend *you were in. It's there on your desk."*

"Thanks, Mom." Mike picked up the magazine. May 1979. He turned to page thirty-eight to look at his old picture: "Mike Despain, 8, Mesa, Arizona, likes to play football and basketball. He wants to be a missionary when he grows up." *He recalled how excited he had been when he first saw it; he'd figured his name was famous all over the world. He closed the magazine and tossed it into his desk drawer. If he didn't get this essay finished pretty soon, his name would be mud.*

ミチナガ

"*Oi,* Matsumoto! Pay attention!" Michinaga snapped upright in his desk. He had dozed off again in his cram school class, and the teacher, Ayukawa-*sensei,* scowled at him from the podium before continuing his lecture. Michinaga glanced at his watch: 9:30 P.M. Just thirty more minutes and he'd be able to go home, eat dinner, then study two or three more hours before going to bed. He sighed at the thought of all the work ahead of him and remembered the students' proverb, "Sleep four hours and pass; sleep five hours and fail."

Next month, March, he'd finally have a chance at the entrance exams. Since the third grade, Michinaga had attended evening cram schools for one—and only one—reason: to prepare for the university entrance examinations. The huge investment of his time and of his parents' tuition money made the very idea of failure horrifying. Michinaga shuddered at the thought. If he failed, his parents would be devastated, but for him it'd be even worse. He would have to live with the shame and disappointment of failure. And he would have to wait a year before taking the tests again, a year filled with part-time jobs, more cram school classes, and countless hours of study. And even then there'd be no guarantee he would pass. Michinaga shook his head. He had no choice: he had to pass those exams.

He stared at the blackboard but was unable to concentrate on the English sentence Ayukawa-*sensei* was diagramming. Tomorrow, Thursday, he had to tell his high school homeroom teacher his final decision about which three universities he would test for. After that, he'd spend the rest of his senior year, most of February and March, cramming for those three exams.

Michinaga looked at his watch again, then at the chalkboard. It was 9:50 and Ayukawa-*sensei* was still explaining the same sentence. *Yo-sho,* what a way to spend a Wednesday night.

マイク

Mike grabbed the rebound and fired an outlet pass to Trey, who was breaking downcourt. A guard from the Alma Twelfth Ward tried to stop Trey's driving layup but ended up fouling him instead. The ball dropped through the net for two points, and Trey went to the free-throw line to shoot for one more.

The buzzer sounded as the players lined up around the key, and Mike saw that Brother Stowell, the priests quorum adviser and juniors basketball coach, had sent in a substitution for him. Alma Twelfth was getting slaughtered, so he didn't mind sitting on the bench for the rest of the game.

The game ended at 9:30 P.M., and afterwards Mike caught a ride home with Brother Stowell. He knew it wasn't a coincidence that no one else was in the car with them. Brother Stowell loved to interview his priests in the privacy of his four-by-four while he shuttled them to and from church, home, or quorum activities.

"So, Mike, you're on the downhill side of your high school career. Three more months of school, then you're a free man. Graduation's what, the first week of June this year?"

Mike nodded. He knew what this was leading to.

"And then what?"

"Huh?"

"I mean what are you going to do with yourself? Work? College?"

"Mission?" interrupted Mike.

"Took the word right out of my mouth." Brother Stowell smiled. "You'll be nineteen in September, so you might want to start getting things ready now. The bishop's in his office every Thursday night for interviews. Maybe

you could drop in tomorrow night and talk to him about working on your mission application."

Mike felt uncomfortable. All his life he had planned on a mission, but now that it was becoming a reality he had some doubts. A mission would mean leaving his friends, his girlfriend, and his new—new to him anyway—car. Then he'd have to put off college for a couple of years, and that would put him behind in the race for engineering school. And on top of everything, or perhaps under it all, was the fact that a mission scared him. With so much at stake, so much to lose, he wondered if a mission would be worth it.

Tonight was as good a time as any to tell Brother Stowell how he felt, but he wasn't looking forward to it. Sheesh, *he thought as he took a deep breath to begin his explanation to Brother Stowell.* What a way to spend a Wednesday night.

ミチナガ゛

Michinaga always liked it when the missionaries visited his seminary class. Brother Nagano was a good teacher, but with Michinaga as the only student, class sometimes seemed a little long. This particular Saturday evening, Brother Nagano had invited two missionaries to attend the weekly seminary class and talk about their experiences.

The four of them discussed missionary work in Japan, the difficulties in presenting the gospel to people who have no Christian background, explaining the Word of Wisdom to people who drink tea with every meal, and finding people willing to listen to the gospel message. "A mission isn't the easiest thing in the world," said the American elder, "but it's an experience I wouldn't trade for anything. I don't know if I've done the Japanese people any good, but my mission sure has changed me."

After class Brother Nagano reminded Michinaga about seminary graduation in two weeks. "Please ask your mother to attend."

"March 12 at the Kobe stake center, right? I think we'll both be there." March 12, the day after his last entrance exam. Things were happening so fast he could hardly believe it. He had taken and failed the first two exams; his last chance was only two weeks away.

Then seminary graduation. The week after that, high school graduation. Of course, seminary and high school graduation paled beside The Last Test. The pressure was nearly unbearable, and Michinaga wondered how he would make it. He didn't know how things would turn out, but he desperately hoped that in April he'd be starting classes in a university, not a cram school.

マイク

Mike slid into his seat just in time to avoid being marked tardy by Brother Mecham. Fifth-period seminary was the pits because he was almost always late. Eating lunch, talking with friends, and doing a page or two of homework left him with barely enough time to get to the seminary building across the street from his high school before Brother Mecham started class. And lately the combined effects of spring fever and senioritis made things even more difficult. School, he decided, should be canceled in spring.

Class was full today; something special must be happening. In the front of the room two missionaries were getting ready to talk to the class. Mike was glad to see them. Not that Brother Mecham wasn't interesting, but seminary five days a week with the same teacher could get a little old. A change of pace livened things up, and besides, he was interested to hear what the elders had to say. Maybe he'd even have a chance to ask them why they decided to go on a mission.

ミチナガ

After placing the white cloth over the four sacrament trays, Michinaga sat down behind the sacrament table in the front of the chapel. It was the first Sunday in April, and he was nervous because he knew—he had known for days—that he would bear his testimony. He wanted to let the ward know what he had been through in the past few weeks.

Looking out over the fifty or sixty people in the chapel, he knew they would understand. Passing a university entrance exam was no small feat. It came as a result of years of high school, cram school, and study, but Michinaga knew it was more than that. Without the help of the Lord, prayer, the ward members, and so many other aspects of the gospel, he never would have made it.

But his joy wasn't complete. At seminary graduation, the stake president had challenged all the young men to serve missions. That stunned Michinaga. He couldn't possibly serve a mission, especially now that he had been accepted by a university. All his life he had prepared for college, and because it would be impossible to take a two-year leave of absence from a university without forfeiting his acceptance, a mission would mean throwing away everything he had worked for. Sure, he could try the entrance exams after his mission, but it would be practically impossible for him to pass any university entrance exam after a two-year layoff. He felt guilty about not serving a mission, but he didn't know what else he could do.

After sacrament meeting he would talk to Bishop Hasegawa about it. Maybe he could offer some advice.

マイク

Two more months, thought Mike as he sat in the darkened chapel watching the satellite broadcast of April general conference, and he'd be finished with high school—and with the priests quorum. He was looking forward to attending the elders quorum, but he'd really miss Brother Stowell. But that was part of life, part of growing up. What had Brother Stowell said that night? Something like, "With age comes responsibility, and with responsibility comes growth."

Yeah, *thought Mike,* that sounds nice, but it doesn't make things any easier. *He would meet with the bishop after this session of conference to talk over the pros and cons of a mission, but he doubted that the bishop would tell him anything he hadn't already heard and didn't already know. Still, he wanted to get this mission thing resolved once and for all and get on with life.*

ミチナガ

Michinaga had talked about a mission to everyone he knew. His homeroom teacher sided with Michinaga's nonmember father. "Only an idiot would give up his place in a university to go on a church mission," he said. "Don't be a fool, Matsumoto." His friends and even one of the local missionaries suggested that he go on a mission *after* he graduated from a university even though it might make it more difficult to get a decent job. His mother's only advice was to talk to the bishop.

Bishop Hasegawa listened silently while Michinaga explained all the reasons why he couldn't go on a mission. "But Bishop, it still bothers me. I thought once I got into a university everything would be easy, but now I'm very confused. Should I serve a mission now or not?"

"Brother Matsumoto, I can't tell you what you should do. It's your decision, and what you decide is between you and the Lord. Maybe you should ask him."

Michinaga did.

Later, his father nearly had a stroke when Michinaga told him that he was going to forfeit his place at the university in order to serve a mission. But after his father calmed down thanks to the soothing words from Michinaga's mother, he managed to give a kind of backhanded blessing. "You've made a terrible mistake, but it's your life, Michinaga-*kun,* and I suppose you can do as you choose. I just hope your brain will work well enough after your mission that you can pass an entrance exam again."

Not exactly encouragement, but not exactly condemnation either. Michinaga hoped to enter the missionary training center in Tokyo in September. The pressure was finally off, and for the first time in months he felt at peace.

マイク

As Mike left the bishop's office, he felt like a huge burden had been lifted. After months of praying, thinking, and talking to his parents, Brother Stowell, and the bishop, he had decided once and for all to serve a mission. It still scared him, but he knew beyond a doubt that it was right.

Next week he'd meet with the bishop again to get his missionary application rolling. If he could arrange it, he wanted to enter the MTC in Provo almost immediately after his nineteenth birthday in September.

Out in the parking lot, he climbed into his car, the car he'd be saying good-bye to, feeling happier than he had felt in a long time.

ミチナガ゛

Michinaga came home from his part-time job as a waiter–cook in a noodle shop not far from his parents' apartment and found only one letter in the mailbox. It had been one of those hot, muggy July days that was even hotter and muggier for Michinaga behind the noodle griddle, and he was exhausted. He snatched the letter out of the mailbox and jogged up the three flights of stairs to his family's apartment.

There were no shoes in the entryway when he opened the front door, so he knew the apartment was empty. He slipped out of his shoes and went straight to the kitchen for a cold glass of *mugicha*, then he sat down on the floor next to the low wooden table in the center of their dining–kitchen area. After a long drink, he looked at the letter. The English return address of The Church of Jesus Christ of Latter-day Saints caught his eye, and he knew immediately what it was.

Inside the envelope were two letters, one in English, one in Japanese. Michinaga placed the English copy on the table and read in Japanese, *Dear Elder Matsumoto: You are hereby called to serve as a missionary of The Church of Jesus Christ of Latter-day Saints. You are assigned to labor in the Japan Sendai mission. . . .*

He laid the letter on the table and gulped down his drink. A mission to Sendai. It was hard to believe it was finally happening. With a mixture of fear and excitement, he realized that in about two months he'd be a full-time missionary. He skimmed the letter again before running through a mental checklist of things left to do before reporting to the Tokyo MTC. Soon he'd be a missionary, tracting, talking to people, teaching the gospel, baptizing. He'd have a partner, of course, a perpetual companion, someone to share the work with, and that would make it easier. Michinaga tried to picture his companion. Maybe he'd be an American.

マイク

The mailbox was almost too hot to touch—in July, the Arizona sun fries everything—so Mike gingerly pulled open the latch and took out the day's mail. With the bundle of letters under his arm, he walked up the driveway to the front door thinking about the cold can of pop waiting for him in the refrigerator. Construction work was murder in the summer, but it paid well and Mike, like everyone else, needed a little extra money. But right now he needed a cold drink.

"I'm home," he called as he walked in the front door. No one answered. He tossed the mail on the kitchen table, pulled a can of pop out of the refrigerator, and dropped into a kitchen chair to savor his drink.

As he sorted through the mail—bills, junk mail, stuff for his parents—he found something addressed to him. It jolted him at first to see The Church of Jesus Christ of Latter-day Saints in the upper left-hand corner. He knew this was it. "Hey, I got my call!" he shouted before he remembered that no one was home.

Dear Elder Despain, began the letter, but Mike's eyes focused immediately on the second sentence: You are assigned to labor in the Japan Sendai Mission.

Sendai, Japan? Where was that? He ran into the family room and pulled the J encyclopedia off the shelf. Japan, Japan. Sendai, he read, a city of 600,000 located in northeastern Honshu, the main island of the Japanese archipelago. Japan? Wow, it was hard to believe. He tried to imagine what it would be like. The language, the people, the culture—it would all be new to him.

Japan. It'd be hard work, no doubt about that, but of course he'd always have a companion, someone to share the work with. He walked back to the kitchen thinking about being a missionary in Japan and wondering about his future companions. Lots of them would probably be Americans, but sooner or later he was bound to have at least one Japanese companion. I wonder, thought Mike as he sat back down at the kitchen table to reread his call, if I'll have anything at all in common with my first Japanese companion. I wonder if he'll have any idea how much I gave up to go on my mission.

An interesting question, but he'd have to wait several months for the answer.

Chris Crowe teaches English at BYU and lives in Provo, Utah, with his wife, Elizabeth, and their four children: Christy, Jonathan, Carrie, and Joanne. In addition to articles and stories for the *New Era,* he is the author of two books for teenagers: a novel, *Two Roads* and a collection of essays, *For the Strength of You.* He has also published a collection of essays for adults, *Fatherhood, Football, and Turning Forty.* He recently completed a literary biography of Newberry Award-winning author Mildred D. Taylor and is now at work on a novel for teenagers.

SARAH'S SECRET

Mari Jorgensen

I KNEW MY MOTHER SUSPECTED something when she tapped on the bathroom door one morning a couple of weeks before Christmas.

"Sarah," she called, "open up for a second, OK? I want to ask you something." My mother's voice was almost drowned out beneath the thumping of the boom box I had perched next to me on the bathroom counter. What now? Here I was in the middle of doing a touch-up job on my roots. I had my hair all clipped into clumps, and I was squirting dye solution at the base of each section, using my plastic-gloved fingers to massage formula 109, "dark chestnut," into the roots. I really didn't need this interruption.

"Just a second," I called back. I was in no mood to face another onslaught of my mother's questions. Was I planning on applying to college? If so, which one? What about the ACT? Where would I live next year? What would become of my piano playing? I was seventeen going on eighteen, and I felt like one of those unsuspecting clowns in old movies, the ones who are minding their own business and suddenly somebody thinks it would be hilarious to rip the rug right out from underneath them. I didn't even want to *think* about next year.

"Sarah, honey?" my mother murmured from the other side of the door. "Please?"

I gave my roots one final squirt of hair dye, peeled the disposable gloves off my hands, and tucked a couple more cotton balls around my hairline. I twisted the volume down on my boom box

118

and cracked open the door. "What, Mom?" I said. "I'm going to be late for school if I don't hurry and get this goop out of my hair."

I gazed at my mother, who was standing in the hallway looking small and shy, like a kindergartner on the first day of school. That was my first clue that she was on to me. My mother has never been a small or a shy person. At five foot nine and after having given birth to seven children—all without a single drop of drugs, mind you—my mother is the epitome of the tireless Mormon home-maker. She should have been the leader of a handcart company. I could just see her out there trudging away on the plains, digging her heels into the muck and putting her shoulder to the wheel and all that pioneer jazz. She'd do whatever it took to protect her religious beliefs and her family.

"I just wanted to ask you something," my mother said again as she reached out and clasped my hands, pulling me into the hall-way with her. Her voice sounded a tad too perky. She rubbed my knuckles with her thumbs. "How would you like a ring for Christ-mas? A ring like the ones I got Miki and Anna two Christmases ago?" My mother twisted my hands in hers as if she were trying to angle them towards the overhead light in the hallway.

That's when I started getting antsy. The fact that my mother was holding my hands at all was strange enough, since we're not much of a touchy family. But the way she was scrutinizing my knuckles like she was a veterinarian looking for fleas—that got me nervous. After all, I wasn't born yesterday. I had seen the talk shows that tell you how to tell if your daughter has an eating dis-order or not. I was pretty sure my mother had seen those same shows, and now she was checking the backs of my knuckles for sores or scars, a definite sign that someone is sticking her finger down her throat in order to induce vomiting. The cat was out of the bag.

"A ring like Miki's and Anna's with Black Hills gold?" I said, forcing my voice to be steady. "That would be cool. But what I'd really like is a wedding ring." I let out a feeble laugh. After all, it could have been that I was just being paranoid. There was a slim chance that my mother really was just sizing up my fingers for a Christmas ring.

A wisp of a smile crept over my mother's lips. I knew what she was thinking: that my knuckles were clean, no sores or scars or anything. "A wedding ring?" she echoed. "You want your mother to buy you a wedding ring?" She chuckled. "Anyway, don't you think you're a little young?"

"Yeah, I guess so." I drew my hands away and started to fiddle with the cotton balls that were threatening to pop out from underneath my headband. I was sure rivers of hair dye would stream into my eyes at any second. That's all I needed: fried eyeballs.

I flashed my mother a smile. Inside I was thinking *safe*. What my mother didn't know was that I always used the handle of a toothbrush to make myself throw up. I was, you see, very careful to avoid any dead giveaways as to what I was doing.

I am not a freak. At the time all this was happening, I was a lot like other high school girls. I had friends. I was my ward's Young Women pianist. I dated guys, although sometimes I felt that if the pickings got any slimmer, I would have to resort to drooling over rock star magazines like the girls with safety pins stuck in their ears who I saw as deeply in need of a life.

The TV is maybe one reason I started making myself throw up. People tell me I look like Courtney Cox, for example, but when I catch her sitcom on Thursday nights all I see is a girl with a body as slim and limber as a licorice whip. I just don't see the resemblance. In fact, I think my mother's pioneer frame is part of why I'm what you would call big-boned. That's a nice way of saying that I'm built like a linebacker. At least that's how I see myself. My mother says that I have a strong, well-proportioned body. *Whatever* is what I say.

I just don't know if I can really pinpoint a time that transformed me from an everyday girl into a label that sounds so whacked-out as *bulimic*. It seems like one day I got fed up with the chunkiness of my thighs, and that's when I started hoarding Buns of Steel videotapes and exercising to them late at night after everyone had gone to bed. I started eating dry cereal for breakfast, too. Pretty soon I was snarfing down Corn Pops—zero grams of fat, low in calories—all the time and swearing off everything else, until I cracked. Then I would do things like swing by McDonald's and devour three orders of supersized fries, a quarter-pounder with cheese, and two hot apple pies.

I made myself throw up for the first time on the night of the McDonald's fiasco. It felt good to be in control again.

I really have no idea what triggered this thing. All I know is that I was sure I would shrivel up and die if anyone found out. I figured my mother would try to pack me off to the funny farm. My two older sisters would peer quizzically at me from the safety of their size-five jeans. My best friend, Angie, would go all melodramatic on me and try to jump in with both feet and save me from myself. And the last thing I wanted was saving.

I met Angie at our locker on the morning my mother cornered me in the hallway next to the bathroom.

"So what are you asking from your parents for Christmas?" Angie inquired as she Oed her mouth in front of the sorry excuse for a mirror we had stuck with a magnet onto our locker door. She outlined her mouth with a brown lip pencil, then started in with her lipstick. In the four years that Angie and I had been best friends, I had never once seen her arrive at school fully together.

"Christmas?" I said as I squeezed by Angie to try and pry my chemistry book out of our locker. "I told my mom I wanted a wedding ring."

"A what?" Angie began to choke like she had just swallowed her tube of lipstick. Like I said—melodramatic.

"Relax," I said. "I was just kidding." I finally managed to yank my chemistry book loose, which was stuffed into the depths of our locker behind a plastic grocery bag full of Angie's gym clothes.

"I hope you're just kidding!" Angie was practically yelling at me. "You and I are going to be roommates at BYU for at least three years before either one of us can get engaged. Remember? We made an oath in ninth grade, and I'm holding you to it." Angie snapped the lid of her lipstick firmly shut—for emphasis.

"I don't know if I can get into BYU," I mumbled. I started to leaf through my chemistry book, looking for any assignments Angie may have stuck into the wrong book. She was prone to doing stuff like that. I usually took a few minutes in the mornings to slip her assignments—which tended to float around our locker like fallen leaves—into her appropriate folder.

"Sure you can get in to BYU." Angie was brushing her hair now, three brusque strokes on either side of her head. "I'll help you with the ACT. You'll breeze through it."

What Angie didn't know is that I have never breezed through anything in my life, especially anything related to school. In fact, what was as easy as breathing to Angie was usually more like an acute case of asthma for me. It's tough being best friends with someone who pulls off almost straight As, especially when you're pretty sure she studies with the same frequency a giraffe dances the polka.

"So, do you have to work tonight?" Angie had her head stuck inside our locker and was rummaging around for something. She stood up clutching a half-eaten bag of salt-and-vinegar potato chips. "Ah, breakfast," she murmured as she uncurled the top of the bag. "Some?" she offered through a mouthful of pure fat and calories.

Since I hadn't eaten my impoverished bowl of dry Corn Pops that morning, those potato chips looked very appetizing. "Thanks," I said, reaching for the bag. "And no, I don't have to work tonight."

"So let's go to Baskin–Robbins and then catch a late movie. What do you say?" Angie flipped her blond bangs away from her face and munched a potato chip.

Suddenly I wasn't feeling so hot. When had my head started to pound? My skull felt like a clenched fist. I shouldn't have popped those three diet pills this morning. "I don't think so," I told Angie. "My sisters are driving home from BYU for Christmas break tonight, and my mom wants us to do something as a family." I tucked my chemistry book under my arm and made like I was going to go to class.

"Oh." Angie grabbed a notebook out of our locker and slammed the door, giving the combination dial a hard twist. She was probably wondering why I wasn't inviting her to our family get-together. Considering the amount of time Angie spent with my family, my parents should have just drawn up the adoption papers and been done with it. But I needed some time to myself; plus, my head was killing me.

"I'm sorry," I said. "It's just that my mom—"

Angie shrugged and gave me a no-big-deal wave of her hand. Then, before I knew what was happening she had stuffed the bag of salt-and-vinegar potato chips into my hands and taken off. As I watched Angie's twiggy figure running down the hall, a loose sheet of paper—probably her assignment for that day—fluttered through the air and settled on the hard tile of the school hallway. I didn't call after her. She'd probably ace her classes anyway, even without that particular assignment. Some people get all the breaks.

Everything after that seems like a bad dream. *Who cares about chemistry?* I remember thinking as I locked myself into one of the stalls of the girls' bathroom with two Twix bars and a large carton of chocolate milk I had gotten out of the school vending machines. *It's not like I'm going to be able to go to college, so why try?* With that thought, I tore into a Twix bar, gulped down the chocolate milk, and polished off Angie's bag of potato chips. Then I stuck the handle of my toothbrush down my throat to make myself throw up everything I had just eaten.

The next thing I knew I was staring up into a set of white lights that I thought were maybe telling me I was in heaven. When the face of Miss Jensen, the school nurse, came into view, I knew that wherever I was it was definitely not heaven.

Stupid. I was so stupid. Nobody knew I had this problem, and no one but my mother really knew how much I struggled with school. If I could have just gotten hold of my life and stopped choking down diet pills and making myself throw up, no one would ever have known about any of this. Now I would probably be the laughingstock of my entire school.

"Sarah?" Miss Jensen was saying.

I squeezed my eyes shut, silently praying for the room to stop spinning out of control long enough for me to make a break for it. Maybe Nurse Jensen hadn't spilled the beans yet. But I knew that was wishful thinking.

"Sarah, your mother is here."

Just as I suspected.

I felt a cool, dry hand slip into mine. I knew it was Mom's.

I opened my eyes and looked up into my mother's face. Her eyes were rimmed with red. She looked at me carefully. "Angie called me," she said. "She followed you into the girls' bathroom to see if you were making yourself throw up. We had our suspicions. And it's a good thing she did follow you. You fainted, Sarah. Your poor body has taken a beating."

Angie? Angie was in on this? I wondered who else besides my mother knew by now. My best friend didn't exactly have the reputation for being able to keep her mouth shut. Maybe they would announce it on the six o'clock news that night.

But somehow as I lay there in the school nurse's office and felt my mother's strong hand in mine, I was relieved. Finally this was not just my secret anymore.

"You scared me," my mother said as she stroked my fingers. My mother's hands were trembling. I had made my tough-as-nails mother afraid? "I don't know how you got to this point," she continued, "but you don't have to do this alone, you know."

I didn't say anything. Flowers of pain still danced in front of my eyes. I was starting to get my bearings a little. As I glanced around the room I could see the fuzzy outline of Angie leaning against the door frame. She kept lifting her fingers to her eyes like she was wiping tears away. Angie was my best friend, but I never knew until that moment how much she loved me.

"OK?" my mother said. "Dad and I are here, and we're going to help you, honey."

"OK," I replied. My head still ached, but I was beginning to feel human again.

I could see through the window of the nurse's office that it had started to snow. Flakes the size of quarters were floating down on the other side of the hazy glass. I used to love snow. Miki and Anna and my brother Mike and I used to make snow forts when we were little. Mom would give us her old thread spools and colored beads to use as decorations around the windows and doors. Our forts usually turned out looking like gingerbread houses.

My mother was always trying to give us stuff to make things seem a little better than they were. "Not everyone learns the same way," she told me once when I brought home my report card. "The way I see it, one of the problems with the public schools is the way they assess only certain types of learners. You, Sarah, are a kinetic learner—you learn by doing things hands-on. That's why you're such a wonderful pianist." She had peered at me from behind the lenses of her reading glasses. Her look had said, *Don't worry; this is only ink on paper.* And she waved my report card in the air like maybe if she were to let go it would sprout wings and fly away forever.

The smells of rubbing alcohol and cough medicine floated around me in the nurse's office. I was lying on some makeshift bed, and the wool blanket somebody had covered me with felt like sandpaper. But for the first time in a long time I felt at peace.

"It's Christmastime," my mother said as she pressed one of her hands to my forehead. "And I want you to know that the best gift you could give me is for you to be happy. I love you exactly the way you are, Sarah."

At least that makes one of us, I thought. *And that's a start.*

Mari Jorgensen lives in Salt Lake City, Utah, with her husband, Steve. She recently earned an M. A. in English from BYU and now teaches writing in the Honors Program at BYU and writes for Heber Valley's newspaper, *The Wasatch Wave.* She published a personal essay in BYU's *The Restored Gospel and Applied Christianity.* Her young adult novel, *The Many Masks of Lizzy Barton,* was a finalist in Delacorte Press's fifteenth annual First Young Adult Novel Contest and is currently being considered for publication by Delacorte. Mari is busy revising this novel and working on her second young adult novel, *My Friend, the Fat Boy.*

Have you ever wondered how great it would be
to be free from rules and parental control?
Wouldn't it be great to live as you want, do what you want?
Nick and Gordon try the free life for a while.
It's not as glorious as they expected.

A LIGHT STILL BURNING

Alma Yates

NICK MARTINDELL SHUT OFF THE engine of his pickup truck and grimly tromped down the dirty concrete steps leading to the basement apartment he shared with his best friend, Gordon. He pulled the screen door open and let it clatter shut behind him. He wrinkled his nose as he reluctantly took a breath of air. Even for late July the air was hot and humid, and the heat in the kitchen was especially stifling, compounding the stale smell of pizza, chips, and unwashed dishes. The apartment was quiet except for the buzz of a dozen fat, lazy flies and the annoying drip of the water faucet.

Bread crumbs littered the table. The trash can in the corner overflowed. A pair of his tennis shoes were lying in the middle of the grimy floor, which hadn't been mopped in more than two months.

He went to the refrigerator, pulled it open, and glared inside. A carton of milk, several slices of bread, a half-stick of butter spotted with bread and jam, a half-jar of mustard, and several wilted vegetables were all he found. He grabbed the carton of milk, smelled it, grimaced, and poured the contents down the sink.

"Gordon," he called out after slamming the fridge door and kicking his tennis shoes under the table, "you home?"

No answer.

Nick walked down the narrow hall leading from the kitchen to the bedroom. He pushed the door open. Two boxes and a suitcase partially blocked his way. Gordon sat on the edge of the bed, which was stripped bare to the mattress. He stared up at Nick without speaking.

"What's all this?" Nick blurted out, pointing at the boxes and suitcase but making no attempt to enter the room.

"I'm leaving," Gordon answered, getting up from the bed. He pulled a bulging canvas bag from the closet and set it on the floor next to the rest of his things. "I wanted to tell you before I left."

"I thought we were in this together. This was your idea too."

"It's no good, Nick," Gordon sighed, "not for me."

"It was good enough for you all last year when we planned it," Nick flared, kicking the boxes aside and coming into the room. "Graduation night that's all you talked about. You were going to break away from Mommy and Daddy and get completely away from all that family stuff. You were going to make it on your own as soon as you turned eighteen. Well, you're eighteen."

"It's just not my kind of life."

"It's freedom. Here we live the way we want to. We come in when we want. We drink and eat when and what we want. Nobody's telling us what to do."

"I guess I didn't realize life away from home could be so glorious."

"It's what we wanted—freedom."

Gordon smiled wanly. "If this is freedom, slavery can't be half-bad."

Nick sneered. "You wanted to be a big man on your own. I guess you found out that someone still had to tuck you in at night and help you say your prayers. All right, what really made you change your mind? I got a right to know. You're copping out on me, leaving me holding the bag."

Gordon met Nick's angry glare. "I was just trying to prove a point. That's all we've ever been doing here—trying to prove a point. I decided the point wasn't worth proving. We were wrong from the beginning."

"And what made you decide that?"

Gordon's cheeks flushed crimson, and he grabbed at a pile of Nick's soiled clothes in the corner. "I'm sick of this," he growled, pushing the clothes under Nick's nose. "I'm sick of yellow sheets that haven't seen water for two months. I'm sick of dirty dishes in the sink. I'm tired of crumbs and pop spilled all over the kitchen floor. I'm sick of a greasy, grimy, dirty, putrid shower. I'm sick of this whole lousy place. What does living like a couple of pigs prove?"

"Clean it if you don't like it."

"It's not that simple. It's not like I thought it would be. I just want to—" He paused and then continued in a quiet voice, "I just want to get out of here. I'm going home." He stooped and picked up a box and his pillow.

"What really made you change your mind?" Nick challenged. "So the place is a mess. You knew it would be. You told me so yourself when we moved in here. You said we'd probably let things get dirty. Well, we did. Now why are you complaining?"

Gordon paused and faced his roommate. "All right. I'll tell you. You know, when we used to plan all this, living away from home and all, I tried to figure out why we were going. You see, I needed a reason. I couldn't just leave. At the time, finding a reason wasn't hard. Mom and Dad were too strict. They didn't understand things. They were always forcing me to do something. There were too many rules. There were lots of bad things about home, and I thought of all of them."

Gordon glanced up at Nick, who scowled. "When we came here," Gordon continued, "I told myself how good it was. I think I believed it then. This was living. We had it made. But there was always something missing. I was kidding myself. Finally I tried to figure out what was missing. I thought about home." He smiled and shook his head slowly. "I began to remember not the bad things, not the things that convinced me to come here. No, I remembered the other things, and there were lots of them. Home isn't so bad, Nick, not half as bad as we've tried to prove."

"You're quite the preacher. They'll have you back in church before long," Nick muttered.

"I've already gone two weeks in a row, priesthood, sacrament meeting, the whole bit."

Nick stared. "I don't believe it."

"You know what, Nick? I liked it."

Nick groaned.

Gordon continued with enthusiasm. "You know, I found out something. I've never liked church. You know why? Because I never gave it a chance. I've never given a lot of things a chance. I'm not saying home and church and all that are for me, because I don't know for sure. I just don't know, not right now. But I tried this way, and this way sure isn't what we cracked it up to be." He waited for Nick to respond, but Nick remained silent.

Gordon slapped the wall with the flat of his hand. "Nick, we're trying to prove the wrong point! What have we got to show for it?" He snatched the dirty laundry and flung it across the room. "All we've got are some dirty jeans, some stale socks, and a crummy, sticky, kitchen. Big deal! I want out. This is—"

"Gordon," Nick interrupted, "you know what? You depress me. In fact, the last couple of weeks I've become depressed every time I've seen you."

Gordon smiled. "Nick, you're always depressed. I don't have anything to do with it. You're just mad at the whole world. One of these days you're going to wake up and find that the world was never mad back and that all this other never proved anything."

"You know where the door is, or do you want me to take you by the hand?" Nick asked angrily.

Gordon shrugged and walked out of the bedroom. Several minutes later he was back for the rest of his things. As Gordon picked them up, Nick asked dryly, "And you're leaving me holding the bag? What about the rent money?"

"There's an envelope on the dresser. It's next month's rent money—all of it, not just half."

The two stared at each other. Neither spoke. Finally Gordon gathered up his remaining things and turned to go.

"Soon they'll be calling you on a mission," Nick laughed sarcastically. "Elder Patrick Gordon Crandell, all decked out in his white shirt and tie and his hair shaved to the skin."

"You know," Gordon replied calmly, "that doesn't sound so bad."

As soon as Nick heard the kitchen door close and Gordon's departing footsteps, he hurled his pillow across the room.

For half an hour Nick laid on his bed. He closed his eyes and tried to sleep, attempting to block the entire day from his mind, but it was too early in the afternoon. Sleep eluded him.

He felt hungry. He went to his dresser, where he kept a supply of candy bars, but he slammed the dresser drawer as soon as he had opened it. He didn't want candy. He was tired of eating candy bars, chips, and cookies. He wanted some real food, something like—but he refused to think of that. That was over, in the past. He wouldn't follow Gordon back. He opened the drawer again, snatched a candy bar, ripped off the wrapper, and crammed the candy into his mouth. No, he wouldn't go back.

He was free here.

He returned to bed but a vague hunger persisted, a nagging desire for something satisfying, something that didn't really have anything to do with food.

Hoping to find relief, Nick crawled from the bed and went to the kitchen. Instead, a flood of nauseating disgust swept over him.

He left the apartment, got into his pickup, and drove nowhere in particular, just someplace, anyplace away from—well, he just wanted to drive, he told himself. He was not running, just leaving for a time.

Soon he found himself out of town, driving into the country along the narrow road that looped around the foot of the mountain and passed through small farms. The road was familiar. He'd traveled it often. It frustrated him that he was driving there now, but he continued. After all, it was just a drive like any other drive. It didn't mean anything.

Five miles out of town he stopped in front of a frame house set back a hundred feet from the road in a grove of elm and poplar trees. The station wagon that usually occupied a place under the giant elm tree was missing. He could tell no one was home.

Nick sat in the truck for several minutes before finally opening the door and stepping out. He looked up and down the highway furtively and then walked across the road to the front door. The door was unlocked. Of course, he knew it would be. They never locked it. He swallowed hard and walked in.

A rich aroma of baked bread lingered in the air. Unconsciously he breathed deeply, feeding hungrily upon the aroma and the memories it inspired.

The kitchen sink was clean. The floor was swept and mopped

to a pleasant glow. The plastic garbage container was empty and free of foul odors. He breathed the clean air and moved about the house, touching the sink, opening the fridge, glancing into the bathroom, sitting momentarily on the sofa to thumb through magazines. He was unable to explain his behavior. It baffled him, yet he felt compelled to linger.

In his reverie he almost forgot the time. Half an hour passed. They would be home soon. Suddenly he realized that he didn't want them to find him here, even though it was just to see. They would misunderstand, see it as a surrender, a weakening.

As he got up from the living room sofa, he noticed his picture hanging on the wall with those of his parents and brothers and sisters. It startled him. The picture's presence seemed so incongruous. He had assumed that when he had walked away, coldly abandoning his family, they would naturally reject him. His picture loudly proclaimed otherwise.

He started for the front door but saw a loaf of homemade bread lying on the table next to a jar of his mother's strawberry preserves, his favorite. A note under the jar read: *Nick, we went to the park for a picnic. Come and join us if you can. We would love to have you with us, but we will understand if you can't. Take the bread and jam. We love you, Mom.*

The note fluttered to the floor. "How did she know?" he whispered angrily, feeling as though he had been observed during his secret visit. He picked up the note and read it again. There was no rebuke, no mention of his weeks of silence, no mention of his absence, his rebellion, his complaining. Merely a quiet, subtle invitation to—but he was not coming back! He crumpled the note. He didn't need them. He would not give them the satisfaction.

He started for the door, leaving the bread on the table, but he stopped before going out. The old hunger returned and coaxed him. He glanced back. Taking the bread didn't mean anything, he thought. A loaf of bread was a loaf of bread. He could buy one at the store if he wanted to. A loaf of bread didn't mean he had given up. So he did come back. It was just a visit. He didn't have anything to do. What was wrong with taking a ride and stopping someplace? He was independent.

He returned to the table and grabbed the bread and preserves. He held them in his hand, pondering. Finally he turned
and left.

Almost an hour after he left, a station wagon pulled under the
elm tree. Doors burst open, and seven children tumbled out and
raced for the house.

An older man and woman stepped from the car. Exhausted
but satisfied smiles touched their lips as they watched their children storm into the house.

The woman was the first to enter the kitchen. As she did, her
gaze went to the kitchen table, as it had done so many times during
the last two months. At first she disbelieved, wondering whether
she had forgotten in her rush to get away to the park. Then she saw
the crumpled note. The bread and the preserves were gone!

Trembling, she sat down at the table and looked up at her husband, who now stood behind her. "I knew it," she whispered. "I
knew he couldn't forget forever."

"It doesn't mean he's coming back," he cautioned. He remembered too well the hurts she had suffered. He didn't want her
snatching at elusive hopes.

She smiled and nodded. "I know," she replied, "but he was
here. For now that's enough."

When Nick arrived at his apartment, he tossed the bread and
preserves on the table and looked in the fridge: still bare and dirty.
Ignoring the bread, he went into his bedroom, turned on the
stereo, and tried to wash away the memory with music.

Angrily he jumped from the bed and began snatching sweaty,
soiled shirts, pants, and socks from the floor and stuffing them
into a canvas bag in the closet. He folded his blanket and pulled
the sheet on his bed tight. Grabbing a T-shirt from his drawer, he
attacked the accumulation of dirt and dead flies on his dresser and
windowsill.

He returned to the kitchen, determined to push the job to its
completion. The dishes went first, and while they dried in the sink
he filled a bucket with water, found a brush and rag, and fell to his
knees on the kitchen floor.

With his jaw clamped tight, he attacked the floor, digging and gouging at the sticky pop stains, the ground-in ketchup and honey spots, and the two months' buildup of dirt and grease. He became oblivious to time.

It was late when he finally stopped. His knees were tender, his arm and shoulder ached, and his fingers were wrinkled. But the apartment was clean. A grim satisfaction was carved upon his brow as he wandered throughout the apartment, surveying his work. However, his satisfaction was short-lived. Though he had succeeded at imitation, the old craving persisted.

He became desperate. He cut himself a slice of his mother's bread and smothered it with strawberry preserves, but when he was finished he was still unsatisfied. There was no escape from the pervasive, lonely depression.

Once more he fled the apartment. This time he didn't encounter a single car as he drove along the familiar country road. As he drove, he ridiculed himself for returning, but he didn't turn back. He lacked the will to rationalize, and his mind was bombarded with memories.

He remembered not the seemingly strict discipline, not the rules he had tried to escape or circumvent, not the arguments, not the usual memories he had conditioned himself to conjure when he was tormented by sentimental reminiscence, but instead he remembered the quiet visits with his father before the contention had started. He remembered how safe and secure he had felt as his father wrapped a strong arm around his shoulders and drew him close. He remembered his mother sitting by his hospital bed for days after his knee operation. There was little she could do, but she was there wiping his brow, holding his hand, and lending him stability in the midst of strange surroundings. He recalled the vocal cheering section that had followed him to all his football and baseball games. He had been embarrassed at the time, but now he yearned to hear those enthusiastic cheers again.

The pickup slowed to a crawl as he neared the house. The station wagon was parked under the giant elm. The house was completely dark. Except for the lone porch light!

I wonder who's still out? he thought. He remembered that the porch light never dimmed as long as one of the family was out. Even when he worked past midnight at Ernie's Café, he had come home to that beckoning porch light.

"And when you come home," his mother had insisted gently, "stop by our room and tell us you're in. I don't sleep well while someone's still out."

Nick looked at his watch. "Almost 3:00 A.M.," he muttered, bewildered. "Teresa can't still be out on a date. Not this late. And Paul doesn't work nights. And none of the little ones would be away."

Suddenly the buried hunger exploded within him, and he knew for whom the light burned, and he knew that during the last two months the light had never been switched off.

Only then did he begin to understand the strange hunger that had plagued him. He knew it had nothing to do with tangibles such as clean sheets, waxed floors, and fresh-baked bread. With a little effort he could duplicate those. There was something else, something far more significant and fulfilling.

His fierce pride prevented him from making any bold concessions this night, but deep within him there was a quiet serenity. There was still a gap between him and them. Having grown and festered over a period of months, it was deep and wide, but as Nick stared at the porch's enduring beacon, he sensed that the gap would be bridged and he could return.

Alma Yates was born and raised in Brigham City, Utah, but presently lives in Snowflake, Arizona, where he works as the principal of Highland Primary School. He graduated from Brigham Young University with a B.A. in English and an M.A. in educational administration. He and his wife, Nicki, are the parents of seven sons and one daughter. In addition to his short stories and articles, he has published six novels: *The Miracle of Miss Willie*, *Horse Thieves*, *The Inner Storm*, *Ghosts in the Baker Mine*, *No More Strangers, Please*, and *Nick*.